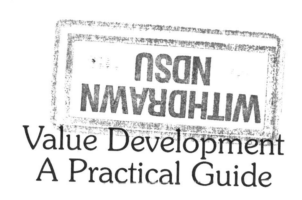

# Value Development
# A Practical Guide

# VALUE DEVELOPMENT
# A PRACTICAL GUIDE

## Janet Kalven, Larry Rosen, Bruce Taylor

PAULIST PRESS
New York/Ramsey

Photo Credits:
   Dale G. Folstad, pages 14, 36, 48, 124
   Paul M. Schrock, pages 64, 76, 148
   Rick Smolan, pages 8, 70, 82, 100

ISBN: 0-8091-2445-9

Library of Congress
Catalog Card Number: 82-81685

Published by Paulist Press
545 Island Road, Ramsey, N.J. 07446

Printed and bound in the
United States of America

# CONTENTS

Foreword ................................. 9

Introduction ............................. 12

**PART I: SKILLS FOR GROWTH**
   A. A Story ........................... 15
   B. The Four Skills .................... 16
      1. Instrumental Skills ............. 16
      2. Interpersonal Skills ............ 20
      3. Imaginal Skills ................. 22
      4. System Skills .................. 27
      Skill and Development ............. 31
      Questions To Be Addressed ........ 34

**PART II: CHARTING ONE'S CONCIOUSNESS TRACK**
   A. Exploratory Exercises ............. 37
      1. Identifying Act and
         Choice Values ................. 37
      2. Personal Values and
         Family Values ................. 39
      3. Ideals and Values ............. 39
   B. Time Diary ....................... 40
      1. Directions for keeping
         a Time Diary .................. 40
      2. Analysis: Time ................ 45
      3. Analysis: Persons ............. 49
      4. Analysis: Daily Perceptions ... 50
      5. Analysis: Feelings ............ 51
   C. Construction of Your Conciousness
      Track ........................... 52
   D. Skills Inventory .................. 55
      1. Instrumental Skills ........... 56
      2. Interpersonal Skills .......... 57
      3. Imaginal Skills ............... 58
      4. Systems Skills ............... 59
      5. Drawing Your Skill Profile .... 60
   E. Designing Your Personal
      Growth Contract ................. 61
      1. Primary Values and Goals ..... 61
      2. Means Values and Objectives .. 62
      3. Writing Your Personal
         Growth Contract ............. 65
   List of Values· ..................... 67
   Phases and Stages of Consciousness ... 69

**PART III: EXCERCISES TO DEVELOP INSTRUMENTAL SKILLS**
   Instrumental Skills .................. 71
   1. Identifying Your Instrumental Skills ... 71
   2. The Tools You Use ............... 71
   3. Developing Decision-Making Skills ... 71

4. Decision-Making Skills . . . . . . . . . . . . . . . . . . 72
5. Decision-Making . . . . . . . . . . . . . . . . . . . . 73
6. Approaches to Risk Taking . . . . . . . . . . . . . . 73
Exercise 4 Answer Sheet . . . . . . . . . . . . . . . . . 74
Exercise 5 Answer Sheet . . . . . . . . . . . . . . . . . 75
7. Moral Choice as an Instrumental Skill . . . . . . . 77
An Ethical Decision-Making Model . . . . . . . . . . . 77

**PART IV: EXERCISES TO DEVELOP
INTERPERSONAL SKILLS**

A. Developing Self-Awareness . . . . . . . . . . . . . . 83
  8. Tuning Into Yourself . . . . . . . . . . . . . . . . 83
  9. Using the Awareness Wheel . . . . . . . . . . . . 84
  Work Sheet: Ex. 9 . . . . . . . . . . . . . . . . . . . 85
  Answer Sheet: Ex. 9 . . . . . . . . . . . . . . . . . . 85
  10. Automatic Writing . . . . . . . . . . . . . . . . . 87
  11. Getting in Touch with
      The Other Side of Your Mind . . . . . . . . . 87
  12. Becoming Aware of Your "Self-Talk" . . . . . 88
  13. Getting In Touch with Your "Core-Self" . . 88
  14. Distinguishing Thoughts and Feelings . . . . . 88
  Worksheet Ex. 12 . . . . . . . . . . . . . . . . . . . 89
  15. Identifying Feeling Statements . . . . . . . . . . 90
  16. A Fantasy Trip . . . . . . . . . . . . . . . . . . . 90
  Work Sheet Ex. 15 . . . . . . . . . . . . . . . . . . . 91
  17. Exploring the Unknown . . . . . . . . . . . . . . 92
  18. Accepting Oneself . . . . . . . . . . . . . . . . . 92
  19. Identifying One's Personality Type . . . . . . . 92
  Observers Check Sheet: Ex. 17 . . . . . . . . . . . 93
  Personal Style Inventory . . . . . . . . . . . . . . . 95
  Personal Style Inventory Scoring Sheet . . . . . . 97

B. Communication Skills: Self-Disclosure . . . . . . . 98
  20. The Johari Window . . . . . . . . . . . . . . . . . 98
  21. Getting Started . . . . . . . . . . . . . . . . . . . 99
  22. Drawing Yourself . . . . . . . . . . . . . . . . . . 99
  23. Describing You, Describing Me . . . . . . . . . 99
  Work Sheet Ex. 21 . . . . . . . . . . . . . . . . . . . 101
  24. Sharing Secrets . . . . . . . . . . . . . . . . . . . 102
  25. Disclosing Negative Feelings . . . . . . . . . . . 102
  26. Acting Out Anger . . . . . . . . . . . . . . . . . . 103
C. Communication Skills: Active Listening . . . . . . 103
  27. Mirroring . . . . . . . . . . . . . . . . . . . . . . . 103
  28. Making Contact with Others . . . . . . . . . . . 103
  29. Receiving Messages . . . . . . . . . . . . . . . . . 103
  30. Perception Checking . . . . . . . . . . . . . . . . 104
  31. Listening Trios . . . . . . . . . . . . . . . . . . . . 104
  32. Dealing with "Mixed Messages" . . . . . . . . . 104
  Work Sheet Ex. 31 . . . . . . . . . . . . . . . . . . . 105
  33. Identifying the Other's Feeling . . . . . . . . . 106
  34. Role Reversal . . . . . . . . . . . . . . . . . . . . 106
  35. Alter Egos . . . . . . . . . . . . . . . . . . . . . . 106
  36. Communicating with Different
      Personality Types . . . . . . . . . . . . . . . . 106
  Work Sheet Ex. 33 . . . . . . . . . . . . . . . . . . . 107

D. Communication Skills:
   Giving and Receiving Feedback . . . . . . . . . . 108
  37. The Gift of Happiness . . . . . . . . . . . . . . . 109
  38. Symbolic Feedback . . . . . . . . . . . . . . . . . 109
  39. A Feedback Experiment . . . . . . . . . . . . . . 109
  40. A First Experience with Feedback . . . . . . . 109
  41. Relationships: A Feedback
      Worksheet . . . . . . . . . . . . . . . . . . . . . 110
  42. Group Sculpture . . . . . . . . . . . . . . . . . . . 110
  43. Seeing Ourselves as Others See Us . . . . . 110
  Work Sheet Ex. 41 . . . . . . . . . . . . . . . . . . . 111
  Observer's Work Sheet Ex. 43 . . . . . . . . . . . . 112
E. Caring and Intimacy . . . . . . . . . . . . . . . . . . 113
  44. An Exercise in Group
      Problem Solving . . . . . . . . . . . . . . . . . 113
  45. Mutual Funds . . . . . . . . . . . . . . . . . . . . 113
  Work Sheet Ex. 44A . . . . . . . . . . . . . . . . . . 114
  Work Sheet Ex. 44B . . . . . . . . . . . . . . . . . . 115
  Work Sheet Ex. 44C . . . . . . . . . . . . . . . . . . 116
  46. Conditions for Developing a
      Relationship to the Level of Intimacy . . . . 117
  47. Exploring Various Definitions
      of Intimacy . . . . . . . . . . . . . . . . . . . . 117
  48. Developing a Personal Credo . . . . . . . . . . 117
  49. Expressing Wants and
      Needs Clearly . . . . . . . . . . . . . . . . . . . 117
  Work Sheet Ex. 47 . . . . . . . . . . . . . . . . . . . 118
F. Dealing with Conflict . . . . . . . . . . . . . . . . . 119
  50. Brainstorming Associations
      with Conflict . . . . . . . . . . . . . . . . . . . 119
  51. Lecturette on Conflict . . . . . . . . . . . . . . . 119
  52. Identifying a Conflict
      Situation . . . . . . . . . . . . . . . . . . . . . . 121
  53. Deciding Whether To Confront . . . . . . . . . 121
  54. How To Confront . . . . . . . . . . . . . . . . . . 121
  55. How to Handle Being Confronted . . . . . . . 121
  A Scribble Sheet for Yourself: Ex. 52 . . . . . . 122
  Ex. 53 . . . . . . . . . . . . . . . . . . . . . . . . . . 123

**PART V: EXERCISES TO DEVELOP
IMAGINAL SKILLS**

Exercises To Free Up the Imagination . . . . . . . . 126
  56. Experiencing the Force of Habit . . . . . . . . 126
  57. The Nine Dots Exercise . . . . . . . . . . . . . . 126
  58. The Poverty Game . . . . . . . . . . . . . . . . . 126
  59. Redefining the Problem . . . . . . . . . . . . . . 127
Exercises for Developing Flexibility . . . . . . . . . . 127
  60. Seeing Squares . . . . . . . . . . . . . . . . . . . 127
  61. Looking at 2 and 2 . . . . . . . . . . . . . . . . . 128
  62. Making Pentaminoes . . . . . . . . . . . . . . . . 128
  63. The Imaginary Ball Game . . . . . . . . . . . . . 128
  64. The Magic Box . . . . . . . . . . . . . . . . . . . 128
  65. Making Fresh Associations . . . . . . . . . . . . 128
Exercises for Developing Fluency . . . . . . . . . . . 129
  66. Observing a Common Object . . . . . . . . . . 129
  67. Developing Alternative Behaviors . . . . . . . 129

68. "Once Upon A Telephone Pole" ........ 129
69. Unusual Uses of a Common Object ..... 129
70. Product Improvement ................. 129
71. Seeing Consequences ................. 129
72. Expressing Alternatives
    through Drawing ..................... 130
Exercises in Synthesis and Elaboration ........ 130
73. Making Up a Story ................... 130
74. Brainstorming ...................... 130
75. Constructing a Game ................. 131
76. Writing a Poem...................... 131
77. Role Playing Specific Situations ........ 132
78. Life Planning ....................... 132

## PART VI: EXERCISES TO DEVELOP SYSTEMS SKILLS

79. Time Management ................... 135
80. Developing a Budget System .......... 137
81. You and Your Systems ............... 138
82. Seeing the System .................. 139
List of Systems: Ex. 81 ................. 139
83. Analyzing Systems .................. 139
84. Developing Vision About
    Systems Change ..................... 141
85. Group Discussion as System .......... 141
Four Types of Classroom
    Organization: Ex. 84 ............... 142
Content Observer Sheet: Ex. 85a .......... 143
Process Observer Sheet: Ex. 85b .......... 144
Role Observer Sheet: Ex. 85c ............. 145
86. Dealing with Systems: Authority ........ 146
87. Applying Assertiveness ............... 146
88. Identifying Group Values .............. 147

## APPENDIX

Learning Summaries ....................... 149
Browsing Bibliography ..................... 156

## Acknowledgements

Champagne, David W. "Personal Style Inventory" in Pfeiffer and Jones, *1980 Annual Handbook for Group Facilitators.* San Diego, University Associates, 1980. Used with permission. Davidman, Leonard, "On Educating the Imagination: A Modest Proposal" in *Phi Delta Kappan*, October 1980. Used with permission. Ford, George A. and Gordon Lippitt, *Planning Your Future: A Workbook for Personal Goal Setting.* San Diego, University Associates, 1976. Used with permission. Koch, Kenneth, *Rose, Where Did You Get That Red? Teaching Great Poetry to Children.* New York, Random House, 1973. Used with permission. ———, *Wishes Lies and Dreams: Teaching Children to Write Poetry.* New York, Vintage Books, 1970. Used with permission. Lyons, Gracie: *Constructive Criticism.* Berkeley: Issues in Radical Therapy, 1976. Used with permission. Miller, Sherod, E. W. Nunnally and D.B. Wackman. *Alive and Aware: How to Improve Your Relationships Through Better Communication.* Minneapolis, Inter-Personal Communication Programs, Inc., 1975. Used with permission. Panzarella, Andrew: *Microcosm, A Radical Experiment in Re-Education for Becoming a Person.* Winona, Minn., St. Mary's College Press, 1972. Parnes, Sidney J., *Creative Behavior Guidebook.* Copyright 1967 by Charles Scribner's Sons, New York, Charles Scribner's Sons, 1967. Adapted with permission of Charles Scribner's Sons. Satir, Virginia, *Making Contact.* Celestial Arts Publishing Company, Millbrae, Cal. 1976. Used courtesy of Celestial Arts Pub. Co. Stevens, John O., *Awareness: Exploring, Experimenting, Experiencing.* Moab, Utah, Real People Press, 1971. Used with permission. Torrance, Paul E., *Torrance Tests of Creative Thinking.* Bensenville, Ill., Scholastic Testing Service, Inc., 1966. Used with permission. Rosenberg, Marshall B., *From Now On.* Sherman, Texas, Center for Non-Violent Persuasion, 1979. Used with permission. Bavelas, Alex: "The Five Squares Problem: An Instructional Aid in Group Cooperation" in the *Journal of the Acoustics Society of America*, 1950. Used with permission. Gordon, Thomas: *Parent Effectiveness Training.* David McKay, New York. Used with permission.

# Foreword

This book, and its companion volume, *Readings in Value Development,* are concerned with value development for today's college student. Therefore, this is a book about self-awareness and personal growth, about feelings, attitudes, choices and skills, about relationships both with one's intimate circle and with the institutions of the larger society.

It proceeds from our conviction that liberal education, to be worthy of the name, must encompass attitudes and values as well as concepts and facts. This is particularly true today in view of the widespread confusion and questioning of values in our culture. In our "global village" with all its possibilities and perils, individuals are faced with acute dilemmas about what to be, what to do, and what to support. These dilemmas are present in all the arenas—personal, professional, national and international—in which we are called upon to act. Today's college students all too often pass through four years of academic training without ever having values issues raised and critically examined. Surely students need to be alerted early in their careers to these questions rather than postpone the confrontation to a time when career and family pressures may not allow for the necessary careful reflection.

As a conceptual focus in dealing with value development, we have adopted the ideas of confluent education as expressed in the work of Brian P. Hall. Confluent value development is at once theoretical and practical, cognitive and affective; it is concerned with all facets of the personality, and offers a set of skills which can be taught and learned in furthering the development of values.

Hall, along with Jean Piaget, Lawrence Kohlberg and others, assumes that in their growth toward maturity, human beings pass through intellectual and moral stages. He also assumes that while humans tend to grow toward both self-fulfillment and the desire to contribute to society, this process is not automatic; that while values are caught rather than taught, nevertheless there are powerful teaching strategies that can be used to foster value development. These strategies include, as priorities, the techniques of self-discovery, the provision of learning environments that encourage growth, and the practice of specific skills.

We can, perhaps, look at the process of value development as a life journey in which the road before us provides a series of unfolding vistas. Until we round the bend, we cannot see the new view. While we might be told by others who have traveled ahead what wonders await us, we cannot really imagine what is in store for us. When we were children, for example, we could not conceive of ourselves as being independent from our parents; even the thought of growing up was sometimes actually frightening! And yet, one day, as we rounded a particular bend in our road, we approached a vantage point which suddenly allowed us to see the possibilities of life beyond the nest. It was challenging and exciting and we couldn't wait to start! Again, as we begin our careers, we find our reward in praise from our supervisor and periodic raises in salary, but the idea that we have the ability to function as the head of the company is not part of our reality. As we grow in competence and experience, however, we may begin to see a leadership role as not only possible but within our purview. At that point another vista is open to us and we are eager to move along once more.

In the Four Phases of Consciousness, Brian Hall has developed a descriptive model that charts a pattern of human moral and intellectual growth in terms of what individuals value in life. He projects a series of four phases through which all humans can pass on their journey toward the fullest possible development. The following chart summarizes his scheme.

As infants, in Phase I, we view the world as chaotic and dangerous. We are concerned with our own survival and preoccupied with the search for warmth, food, and self-delight. As teenagers, if we have had a relatively secure home life, we become less concerned with daily survival and much more concerned with dealing with authority, receiving praise for what we can do, and being accepted by others (Phase II). As adults, if we are to grow in power as persons, we have to move beyond seeking the approval of others into a phase of self-direction, which allows us to enjoy the independent exercise of our powers in shaping the world around us (Phase III). Here we decide for ourselves what is worth doing without being overly concerned about recognition or status. Finally, if we succeed in internalizing the values of Phase III, we can move to the final phase of our journey, a phase which most of us can only dimly imagine. Here we are concerned not just with our own projects, but with joining others in working for the maximizing of human potential and the harmony of human beings with each other and with the environment on a global scale.

By identifying our values and using Hall's Consciousness Track, we can chart where we are on our

# The Four Phases of Consciousness

| ELEMENTS | PHASE ONE | PHASE TWO | PHASE THREE | PHASE FOUR |
|---|---|---|---|---|
| How the WORLD is perceived by the individual. | The world is a MYSTERY over which I have NO CONTROL. | The world is a PROBLEM with which I can COPE. | The world is a PROJECT in which I must PARTICIPATE. | The world is a MYSTERY for which WE must CARE. |
| How the individual perceives its SELF to FUNCTION in the world. | The self EXISTS at the center of a HOSTILE WORLD. | The self DOES things to succeed and to belong in a SOCIAL WORLD. | The self ACTS on the CREATED WORLD with conscience and independence. | Selves GIVE LIFE to the GLOBAL WORLD. |
| What HUMAN NEEDS the self seeks to satisfy. | The self seeks to satisfy the PHYSICAL NEED for food, pleasure, shelter. | The self seeks to satisfy the SOCIAL NEED for acceptance, affirmation, approval, achievement. | The self seeks to satisfy the PERSONAL NEED for being one's self, directing one's life, owning one's ideas. | Selves seek to satisfy the COMMUNAL NEED for global harmony. |

journey and project a future direction. What enables us to take further steps on the journey? The values we are able to perceive and desire are limited by the phase of consciousness we have reached. Remember the image of the bend in the road. Until we reach that vantage point, we simply cannot see what lies ahead. Similarly, a person at a Phase II stage of consciousness cannot perceive Phase IV values. The shift in consciousness that allows a new vision to appear on the horizon becomes possible if certain conditions are met:

1. an environment which supports the person's efforts to internalize the values of the present stage of development;

2. the full internalization of the values of the present stage (needs which are met no longer motivate; values which are internalized no longer suffice as sources of meaning, but dispose the individual to look for new meanings);

3. exposure to role models, whether in life or in literature, who are at a further stage of development and are therefore able to stir new aspirations in the person;

4. a degree of self-awareness about one's feelings, desires, aspirations and choices.

At this point, skill development becomes crucial to growth. To turn the ideals into reality, to translate the new aspirations into consistent behavior, requires skills. This book, as a practical guide to confluent value development, begins with "Skills for Growth," a chapter which relates the Phases of Consciousness to the four skill areas. (The further development of the theoretical framework for the phases of consciousness and the stages of growth will be found in the companion volume, *Readings in Value Development*.)

Hall distinguishes the skill areas as follows:
*Instrumental skills:* the abilities that enable one to get a job done; the intellectual and physical competencies that enable one to shape both ideas and the immediate external environment. They include physical dexterity, handicraft ability, professional and technical expertise, and cognitive accomplishments from the basic three R's to the most sophisticated analysis.
*Interpersonal skills:* the ability to perceive self and others accurately, in ways that facilitate communication, mutual understanding, cooperation and intimacy. These skills are necessary for the development of satisfying human relationships.
*Imaginal skills:* that blend of fantasy and feeling that enables us to combine images and ideas in new ways, to see alternatives, to change conventional ways of doing things, to remedy deficiencies.
*Systems skills:* the ability to see the various parts of a system as they relate to the whole and to plan and design systemic changes.

In order to change both our behavior and our values, it is necessary to practice the various skills needed to function at the next higher stage than the one on which we find ourselves. We know, for example, that for young people to internalize a sense of self-worth and self-confidence, they need to develop ways to get along with each other, to be accepted as belonging to the peer group, and also to be accepted and approved by those in authority. All these behaviors require interpersonal skills. If we take a closer look at some of these skills, we can think of them as value-related. For example, we know it is important to hold our tempers and not lose our heads at the first sign that someone disagrees with our opinions. This is a skill, but it is also a value—that is to say, it is considered a good character trait by those with whom we associate. Thus, we come to value self-control as well as to practice the skill of self-control.

Again, if we are to grow, let us say, from Phase II to Phase III, we first need to feel comfortable at Phase II. At this phase we need to be competent, and therefore must achieve the basic instrumental skills required in this culture, e.g., reading, writing, computation. We value these in themselves, but they also lead to self-confidence, recognition from teachers and parents, and graduation diplomas. Once these needs are met, we can begin to move toward the independence and creativity characteristic of Phase III.

The book then proceeds to a diagnostic section which will enable readers to place themselves in terms of the phases and stages of consciousness. In thus charting one's "Consciousness Track," the individual can see which values have already been internalized, which are in the process of being acquired, and which define one's ultimate aspirations. Another diagnostic instrument, the skills inventory, enables the reader to draw a profile of present levels of development in the four skill areas. All the various exercises in section two are intended to present the individual with new data about the self and also with a series of choices crucial to the process of giving direction to one's life. After working through these materials, the person is in a position to draft a personal growth plan which takes into account individual strengths and limitations, preferences, beliefs, values, attitudes and skills.

Since skill development is crucial to making changes in behavior and values, the remainder of the book is devoted to a series of exercises in each of the four skill areas.

We believe that the experience of wrestling with the clarification of one's own values and seeing the links in one's daily life between behavior, skills and values is vital to a sure grasp of the theory. Ultimately, for a successful process of growth, we must grasp the theoretical framework in all its analytic complexity. Each exercise concludes with a reflective section which poses questions designed to encourage the participants to conceptualize their experience and to reflect critically and creatively upon it. In the final section of the book, we have included a format for writing "Learning Summaries," which we have found a useful device for stimulating the process of reflection. Finally, the theoretical chapters in the *Readings* volume can be used to draw together the various concepts and insights into a more systematic whole.

Special thanks are due to our students and workshop participants at the University of Dayton, Edison State College and Grailville Conference Center with whom many of the exercises in the book were first tried and whose comments have contributed to sharpening the focus of these materials. We also are grateful to Dr. Leroy Eid of the University of Dayton for his support of this project, to Kenneth Groff for his pioneering work with values exercises and to Linda Mc Kinley for her careful work in typing and proofreading the manuscript.

*Janet Kalven*
*Larry Rosen*
*Bruce Taylor*
*University of Dayton, July 1981*

# Introduction

## Suggestions for the Users of These Materials

We have tried to make these volumes useful for the individual who either alone or with a group of friends wishes to undertake a journey of personal growth, and for the facilitator of workshops or other groups in an informal setting, as well as for the classroom teacher.

### FOR THE INDIVIDUAL USER:

We would recommend the following sequence:

1. Chapter I of *Readings in Value Development,* on "Personal Value Clarification" and its importance.
2. Chapters 4 and 5 of *Readings* on "The Four Phases of Consciousness" and the course of "Value Development."
3. Section I of *Value Development* on "Skills for Growth."
4. Section II of *Value Development* on "Charting One's Consciousness Track." In working through the exercises in this section, you will be able to clarify your present values, chart your consciousness track, draw your skill profile, and outline a plan for personal growth.
5. In the light of your personal growth plan, you can look through the ninety or so exercises in the four skill areas and choose those that seem best suited to your needs. Generally, it is better to do a few exercises thoroughly rather than attempt to sample a wide range.
6. Finally, you can choose from the *Readings* the chapters that relate most closely to your interest areas.

### FOR THE TEACHER OR GROUP FACILITATOR:

In working with a group, we recommend following much the same approach as that outlined above for the individual user. We believe that insight into values and value development proceeds from the particular to the general, from the individual's own immediate concerns to the more universal grasp of values and their theoretical implications. You may want to work back and forth between the initial value clarification exercises and the conceptual framework of the phases of consciousness and the stages of growth. The "Time Diary" then leads directly and personally into the value questions that participants are facing in their daily lives, and, together with the skills assessment, can en-

able group members to fashion their own personal growth plans. The facilitator will then be in a position to choose exercises that meet the needs of the majority of group members, and also to recommend to individuals exercises for their specific needs.

Each exercise has been written to include the following components:

1. *A statement of objectives,* indicating the relationship of the exercise to the building of specific skills. In working with a group, it is important to provide a brief theoretical rationale for each exercise, since many people will not invest themselves in the experience unless their need for understanding its relevance is satisfied. Materials useful for this purpose will be found in the introductions to the various exercise sections and to some of the individual exercises.
2. *An activity,* intended to involve the participants experientially. This emphasis on active participation in the learning process accords with our assumption that education has too often neglected the importance of discovering our own truths in favor of memorizing the "facts" put forth by others. Direct experiential learning becomes truly owned, or as one student has said, "Feeling is believing."
3. *An opportunity for sharing* observations, feelings, reactions and insights.
4. *Discussion questions* to sharpen observations and to stimulate reflection on the meaning of the experience and its connection to other experiences and ideas.

Our approach is experiential; the model is essentially an action/reflection model. This makes it all the more important that teachers or facilitators experience the exercises themselves before attempting them with a group. Of course, the more fully the facilitators have grasped the conceptual framework contained in these two volumes, the more easily they will be able to focus specific exercises in a productive way.

The attitude of the facilitator sets the tone for the group. If you as facilitator do not really believe in the exercise, neither will the group. Your conviction and enthusiasm will carry the group along with you; however, it is also wise to avoid raising expectations too high. What you communicate, verbally and non-verbally, in the first few minutes is the single most important element in creating a group climate of openness and trust. Therefore:

- Pay attention to the physical set-up. If you want the group to interact, seats need to be arranged around a table or in a circle so that everyone can see and speak to everyone else without having to turn around.
- If you want persons to share with each other person-to-person, it is usually helpful to establish a first-name basis for everyone, including the facilitator or teacher.
- Be conscious of the inclusion dynamics in the first five minutes of a group meeting. It is often useful to use a simple warm-up exercise which requires each member of the group to say a few words.
- If you want group members to share their feelings honestly with the group, you will need to model this behavior by sharing your own feelings, thus making it legitimate to talk about personal feelings, even in a college classroom.
- With just a few exceptions (e.g., the first few exercises on "breaking set" in the imaginal section), there are no right or wrong answers to the exercises. The aim is to encourage people to voice what they perceive and feel.
- The more you can model the skills and the values, the better.

In dealing with the development of imaginal skills, it is particularly important to create a supportive atmosphere that gives encouragement to free associations and "wild ideas." It is often difficult for teachers, accustomed to dealing with convergent thinking and with problems that have one correct solution, to cope with a range of divergent responses. You may need to deal with your own feelings about "losing control of the group." It is important to separate the brainstorming from the evaluative phases of any activity, and to scrupulously avoid passing judgment until the final stage of the process.

While we emphasize participation of all group members in the exercises, we recognize that a group sometimes contains a disinterested individual who simply does not want to participate. Do not urge such individuals; let them play an observer role. There may also be some over-participators who are looking for an artificial emotional stimulus through group activities. It is wise not to let them dominate a group. Sometimes participation will become such a strong group norm that the group may try to pressure an individual who is disturbed or in a panic at the thought of a particular exercise. Most people know their own limits; it is important to respect these and to leave a face-saving way for them to bow out. One can always learn something by watching.

One exercise at each meeting is all that most people can digest. Too many structured exercises run one after another tend to confuse participants and to prevent the learning from sinking in. It is very important to allow sufficient time for processing both the feelings and the learnings. Encourage group members to express and, if possible, to resolve any feelings that may have been evoked by the exercise.

A trained facilitator is always useful to a group, but in certain exercises we have made a point of listing the facilitator as a necessary resource for a given exercise. In a few cases, as in brainstorming, some previous experience greatly increases the productivity of the exercise. However, in most cases, in listing the trained facilitator we wish to alert the user that the exercise is apt to lead into an emotionally charged situation. It is therefore necessary that the facilitator be experienced enough to be able to aid members both to express their feelings and to come to a degree of closure with the episode.

Ask the group to give you feedback on the usefulness of the experience, either through the use of simple, anonymous reaction sheets, or through a closure circle in which each participant voices one positive and one negative evaluation of the session. Such feedback can be very useful in enabling you to alter your presentation to make the exercises more dynamic, relevant and helpful.

# PART I:
# SKILLS FOR GROWTH*

## A. A Story

Many years ago in a distant land lived two cave dwellers, Wugga and Chug. They spent their days wandering through forest and meadow, gathering roots and berries, climbing trees to take the eggs from birds' nests, eating when they were hungry and sleeping under the stars.

One day, while they were out foraging, a terrible storm came up: the lightning flashed, the thunder roared, the cold rain pelted down. They saw a cave high up on the mountainside and ran for cover. When the storm had passed, Chug noticed that a tall tree, which had been toppled by the storm, was smoldering. Chug and Wugga drew near; it was warm by the tree and felt good after the chilling rain. Chug picked up a stick and cautiously began to poke at the fire. In a few moments, his stick burst into flame. He carried it back to the cave, and he and Wugga soon learned how to keep a fire going with dry sticks and leaves.

Some months later, little Sug was born. Wugga nursed him and made a nest of soft grass for him to sleep on. She dared not leave him alone in the cave when she went out food-gathering, but it was hard to work and carry the baby too. If only I could carry more than one handful at a time, she thought. A picture of a bird's nest flashed through her mind. Gathering some vines, supple twigs and long grasses, she began to plait and twist them together. Soon, she had a rough basket in which to carry a quantity of roots and nuts. Some of the smaller nuts slipped through the cracks, so she began to coat the inside of the basket with mud and leaves. One day, a basket fell into the fire, and before Wugga could rescue it, the vines and grasses burned away, leaving a rough earthenware pot. Wugga was excited. She gathered more clay, shaped several pots and hardened them in the fire. Now she had a way to carry water.

Still, the spring with the clear fresh water was far away from the cave. It would be nice to be close to the spring. As she thought about this, Wugga suddenly imagined a kind of giant basket upside down in the little clearing next to the spring. She told Chug about her idea. At first, Chug pooh-poohed the idea: it was impossible to build such a big basket; besides they were safe in the cave, even if it was small and damp. But Wugga held on to her dream. Another child was born, and Chug brought home two wolf puppies whose mother he had killed in the hunt. The cave really was crowded. Finally, Chug was persuaded, and the couple began work beside the spring, cutting slender saplings with their stone scrapers, setting them in holes in the ground, weaving them together with vines, and plastering the whole beehive shape with clay, until they had a snug shelter.

One evening, as they were sitting around the fire, finishing a pot of squirrel stew, a little band of shaggy primitives appeared. They advanced toward the hut, brandishing their clubs and demanding that Chug and Wugga vacate their house.

Ever the fast thinker, Chug meekly told them the house was theirs, but warned them that it wouldn't be too long before others with superior weapons would take the house from them. War with its accompanying atrocities would be unavoidable. Chug suggested that their futures would all be brighter if they joined hands and forged ahead together. He and Wugga offered to help them build their own houses, adding that a well-placed and fortified wall would discourage unwelcome visitors with ignoble intentions.

And so they founded the first city and called it Chuwuggatown; Chug was recognized as headman and he and Wugga played a major role in the community councils. They distributed the work loads according to individual inclinations and community needs. Wugga showed the women how to make baskets and pots, how to grow grains and vegetables, how to tan the hides of animals for clothing. Chug led the hunters and became expert at hardening spears in the fire; some men in the community took on the care of the flocks. But eventually, because of a considerable population expansion, the need arose for more elaborate tools and more complex human social institutions. A group of lawmakers were selected and a judicial system established. The religious celebrations became the province of a special group, as did the telling of the history of Chuwuggatown.

---

*By Brian Hall and Janet Kalven

15

# B. The Four Skills

Thus, in a matter of a few years, Chug and Wugga and their friends had come a long way. From a group of cavedwellers, they had become more or less sophisticated city people. In the process, they had acquired many new skills, skills upon which all human development depends. These skills fall into four general areas:

1. Instrumental skills
2. Interpersonal skills
3. Imaginal skills
4. System skills

As we explore each of these areas in some detail, it will become apparent that there is some overlap from one area to another. The lines of division are not all that clear-cut, but there is something distinctive about each skill area that prevents this fourfold arrangement from being completely arbitrary.

A look at child development will show us how closely the different skill areas are related. At birth, the human infant has the potentiality to develop all the skill areas. In the first year of life, the rudiments of the first three skill areas are already being laid down. Thus, the newborn begins immediately to develop instrumental skills, e.g., the skills of grasping and holding onto an object, of turning over and sitting up, crawling, walking, and talking. At almost the same time, for babies are born into a network of human relationships, the infant begins to respond to other people. The parents cuddle their offspring, speak or sing to the child, and soon are rewarded with a smile or a laugh. Long before they are a year old, most babies show signs of considerable interpersonal awareness and are quite skillful in making their needs known and getting them met. Imaginal skills are present in germ in the childhood experiences of self-delight and wonder—hence they are indicated by dotted lines in Diagram 1. They begin to develop as the child starts to draw, to build, to play "let's pretend," but can only come to full development in Phase 3 when the autonomous individual values her or his creativity and expresses it freely. System skills are the last to develop, for they require all the other skills together with the ability to handle high levels of abstract analysis, to synthesize complex data from diverse sources, and to project alternatives into a distant future. Diagram 1 illustrates this developmental process.

## 1. Instrumental Skills

Chug exhibited instrumental skills in starting a fire. Wugga showed her instrumental skills in making baskets and pottery, not to mention her verbal and interpersonal skills in persuading Chug to join her in building their hut.

Recently a pilot film for a planned series entitled *Movin' On* appeared on TV. The story revolves around the adventures of two truck drivers with sharply contrasting approaches to life. The one is a beefy, highly physical character in his late forties or early fif-

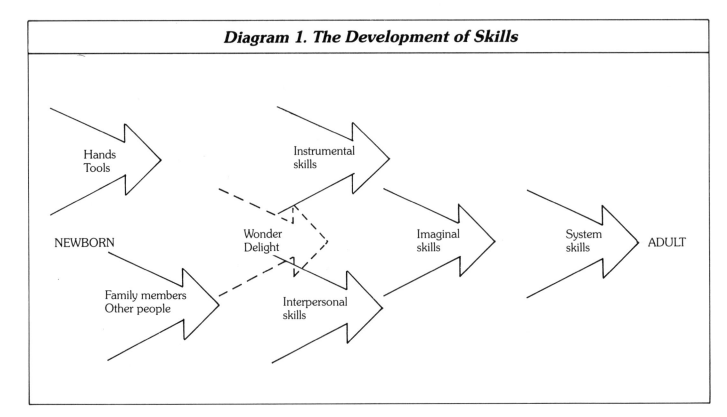

**Diagram 1. The Development of Skills**

Hands
Tools

Instrumental skills

NEWBORN

Wonder
Delight

Imaginal skills

System skills

ADULT

Family members
Other people

Interpersonal skills

ties. He first appears smacking his lips over a cup of coffee at a truck stop while waiting for a waitress to finish her work so he can spend an hour or so with her. The other driver is a young graduate of an Eastern law school who opposed the war in Vietnam and is driving trucks while he tries to find himself.

At one point in the story, the two drivers have contracted for a job that includes a $100 bonus upon safe delivery of the cargo. When they fulfill their end of the bargain and arrive safely at their destination, they are informed that no bonus will be paid. The inclination of the older man is to beat the $100 out of the welcher. But the younger intervenes and obtains the $100 by threatening court action in highly technical legal language.

Each driver has a different set of instrumental skills (coming from distinct phases of consciousness) on which to rely in this conflict situation. In this instance, moral force proved more effective than physical force. But both the ability to fight and the ability to analyze the business transaction in legal terms are instrumental skills.

Instrumental skills are task oriented. They encompass all those abilities an individual can rely on to get jobs done. They cover the very general skills needed by nearly everyone in a given culture, like reading and writing in the United States or hunting and food gathering in some primitive societies. Highly professional or specialized skills like truck driving, using a pipet in chemistry or performing brain surgery are also instrumental skills. Both the designing and using of tools are instrumental skills. This presents us with the following break down of instrumental skills:

1. General skills—such as reading or making change.
2. Professional skills—such as ballet dancing or practicing law.
3. The design and use of tools.

Of course these skills can be divided in other ways, as, for example, bodily and mental skills. We have selected this particular division because it is so serviceable within a developmental framework.

## ENTRY LEVEL SKILLS

Unless persons master those general skills expected of members of a particular society and culture, they cannot be said to fully belong. Indeed without those basic entry skills the achievement of a sense of self-worth will suffer a severe setback. These general skills represent the minimum expectations a society builds into its culture. This is made visibly explicit in the puberty rites of some primitive societies, ceremonies that are the ritual certification that the initiates are qualified skillwise to function as adult members of the tribe.

Certification by a school or successfully passing through an apprenticeship serves much the same function in technological societies, though without the religious overtones of primitive ritual.

## PROFESSIONAL OR SPECIALIZED SKILLS

The sense of belonging and self-worth are also enhanced by the acquisition of more specialized skills. A professor of history belongs to a very select group and can be confident that this peculiar specialty is not typical of the general populace. The same can be said of a plumber.

But professional skills also empower a person to be more independent than others who must cope with life without these exceptional skills. The competence that professionals attain frequently frees them from the worries and concerns typical of someone whose basic aim in life is to meet the expectations of others. The same thing is not true of skills like reading and writing, which are maintenance skills. All we are asserting here is that, all other skill development being equal, the special competence that accompanies the acquisition of professional skills opens the door to existence at Phases III and IV in a way that is not true of the more general instrumental skills.

## THE DESIGN AND USE OF TOOLS

The skill to use tools can be a simple or a highly sophisticated art as Ivan Illich indicates:

I use the term "tool" broadly enough to include not only simple hardware such as drills, pots, syringes, brooms, building elements or motors and not just large machines like cars or power stations. I also include among tools productive institutions such as factories, which produce tangible commodities such as cars and electric current, and production systems for intangible commodities such as "education," "sick care," "conflict resolution" or which "make" decisions. I use the term "tool" for lack of any other which would be equally general and simple.[1]

Not everyone is equally qualified to use all the tools described by Illich. Phase IV persons must have the ability to design and use tools that meet the needs for construction of the ideal world as perceived in their vision of the future. This is beyond the reach of a person whose capabilities are strained by using a hammer or screwdriver or reading the newspaper. It is especially in the designing of human institutions which promote the values typical of Phases III and IV that highly skilled people are required.

Thus, these three categories of instrumental skills are all developmental. Nearly everyone may have the ability to verbalize, but no one would claim that every verbalizer has equal ability. The same can be said of any instrumental skill. They all admit of degrees and are always open to further development.

For centuries, education has emphasized instrumental skills as the key to what is human. Our growth in cognitive abilities, the application of thought to the making of tools, and the expansion of various personal skills constitute the history of the development of civilization.

An instrumental skill is no more than the manner by which we utilize our tools. At one level an individual has skill in using the hammer. Hands and brain coordinate the maximum use of "the instrument called hammer." Skill then is a coordinating function.

At a more sophisticated level the director of a hospital has "skills" in the use of the tool "medicine," coordinating laboratory, doctors, radiology, nurses, and office staff and many other elements into a single efficient instrument.

## TOOL MAKING

Let us look a little more deeply into three processes involved in tool making:

1. Miniaturization
2. Objectification
3. Change of Consciousness

It is through this basic process that tools have always come into being.

Let us take Wugga as an example and see how it works. She is carrying the baby and a handful of roots toward the cave, wondering whether Chug has caught anything on the hunt. If not, they will both be hungry and she will have to make a long trip back to the berry patch and the nut trees. She thinks of the bird nest she has seen and of the eggs laying in the nest. Suddenly, she has a terrific idea: she will make something like the nest in which she can carry nuts and fruit. She has never seen a basket. Where did the idea come from? Briefly, I am suggesting that having assimilated a host of sensory impressions and reflections over a period of time, and being spurred on by a need, she miniaturizes all the data through an intuitive act into the one new idea—basket.

What separates human beings from the animals is this intuitive factor, what we might call reflective intellect whereby we are able to collect data, fantasize, think (reflect) and synergetically come up with new ideas. When any mass of data is assimilated within the small confines of the human mind into a *new* integrated whole, we call that process "miniaturization."

But human beings as the tool makers have always had the capacity to objectify this miniaturized form from the mind into the environment. Wugga wove the basket. Wugga and Chug wove the walls of the much larger basket which became their house. They were able to take the idea inside themselves and then shape the external environment according to it. This is objectification.

All tools, whether they are hammers and saws, houses and office complexes, or social organizations like medicine, law or schools, are objectifications of human ideas projected into the environment in the form of "tool." Paolo Soleri speaks of the process as follows:

The brain has compressed (miniaturized) the "universe" in a few pounds-inches of space-matter-energy. Only by way of this miraculous contraction of performances (information, communication, etc.) is the brain a concrete process presiding over the other miniaturized "universe" of the body.[2]

This then is a life process. Concretely in human social history, complexity is reduced (miniaturized) to ideas in our inner world and shaped into tools in our external world (objectified).

We are social animals; we cooperate and exchange these ideas across generations and cultures. In this we are unique again. Two people with a set of mundane ideas can come up with a third and brilliant thought. Social complexity is miniaturized. Ideas are put together with new data to form an hypothesis that is tested with further data and made into a scientific law.

Through discovering and utilizing laws of science and social organization, we create inventions and govern societies. My point: Miniaturization, objectification, indeed "tool making" change consciousness.

*Miniaturization makes complexity small. This idea is then expressed outwardly as a tool that in turn causes an explosion of consciousness, bringing about even greater complexity, that someone will miniaturize again. This is the developmental process of tool making.*

Tools are also expressions of human moral development, because they can either provide security and love or, if turned to war and killing, can foster fear and mistrust. Moral choice itself is an instrumental skill as Lawrence Kohlberg has shown.

## MORAL CHOICE: AN INSTRUMENTAL SKILL

The ability to arrive at and apply criteria for measuring the morality of a person's behavior exercises cognitive skills that are basically instrumental. Kohlberg has demonstrated that these skills are developmental, the criteria changing as the person develops. Such development follows inevitably as a person's world view and consciousness expand. Any cognitive skill that deals with values must necessarily adjust itself to the needs that assume prominence in the subject's current world view.

So from our perspective, the following schema of moral development by Lawrence Kohlberg constitutes a model of an expanding cognitive instrumental skill that at any stage expresses one aspect of the person's world view.

## DEFINITION OF MORAL STAGES

### I. Preconventional Level

At this level the child is responsive to cultural rules and labels of good and bad, right or wrong, but interprets these labels either in terms of the physical or the hedonistic consequences of action (punishment, reward, exchange of favors) or in terms of the physical power of those who enunciate the rules and labels. The level is divided into the following two stages:

*Stage 1:* The punishment and obedience orientation.
The physical consequences of action determine its goodness or badness regardless of the human meaning or value of these consequences. Avoidance of punishment and unquestioning deference to power are valued in their own right not in terms of respect for an underlying moral order supported by punishment and authority (the latter being stage 4).

*Stage 2:* The instrumental relativist orientation.
Right action consists of that which instrumentally satisfies one's own needs and occasionally the needs of others. Human relations are viewed in terms like those of the marketplace. Elements of fairness, of reciprocity and of equal sharing are present, but they are always interpreted in a physical pragmatic way. Reciprocity is a matter of "You scratch my back and I'll scratch yours," not of loyalty, gratitude or justice.

### II. Conventional Level

At this level, maintaining the expectations of the individual's family, group or nation is perceived as valuable in its own right, regardless of immediate and obvious consequences. The attitude is not only one of *conformity* to personal expectations and social order but of loyalty to it, of actively *maintaining,* supporting and justifying the order and of identifying with the persons or group involved in it. At this level there are the following two stages:

*Stage 3:* The interpersonal concordance or "good boy-nice girl" orientation.
Good behavior is that which pleases or helps others and is approved by them. There is much conformity to stereotypical images of what is majority or "natural" behavior. Behavior is frequently judged by intention— "He means well" becomes important for the first time. One earns approval by being "nice."

*Stage 4:* The "law and order" orientation.
There is orientation toward authority, fixed rules and the maintenance of the social order. Right behavior consists of doing one's duty, showing respect for authority and maintaining the given social order for its own sake.

### III. Postconventional, Autonomous or Principled Level

At this level, there is a clear effort to define moral values and principles that have validity and application apart from the authority of the group or persons holding these principles and apart from the individual's own identification with these groups. This level again has two stages:

*Stage 5:* The social-contract legalistic orientation, generally with utilitarian overtones.
Right action tends to be defined in terms of general individual rights and standards that have been critically examined and agreed upon by the whole society. There is a clear awareness of the relativism of personal values and opinions and a corresponding emphasis upon procedural rules for reaching consensus. Aside from what is constitutionally and democratically agreed upon, right is a matter of personal "values" and "opinion." It is the result of an emphasis upon the "legal point of view" but with an emphasis upon the possibility of changing law in terms of rational considerations of social utility (rather than freezing it in terms of stage four "law and order"). Outside the legal realm free agreement and contract is the binding element of obligation. This is the "official" morality of the American government and the Constitution.

*Stage 6:* The universal ethical principle orientation.
Right is defined by the decision of conscience in accord with self-chosen ethical principles appealing to logical comprehensiveness, universality and consistency. These principles are abstract and ethical (the Golden Rule, the categorical imperative); they are not concrete moral rules like the Ten Commandments. At heart they are universal principles of justice, of the reciprocity and equality of human rights and of respect for dignity of human beings as individual persons.[3]

At Kohlberg's sixth stage, right is defined by the decision of conscience in accord with self-chosen ethical principles that are universal and consistent. This schema carries the individual into our Phase III, after which a new criterion begins to operate, the individual's vision of a new world. Here traditional concepts of justice give way to a vision of the future that, while structured by justice's demands, makes the not yet existing world, the ideal, the new norm of morality. The imaginative resources of the individual and values like harmony, synergy and interdependence become the sources of moral imperatives through the development of constructive tools. The demands of justice that emerge from the already existing world cede their normative role to the basic requirements for the construction of a not-yet-existing human community characterized by the values typical of Phase IV.

In other words, the dominant note of the moral norm of this new level of consciousness is a vision of the future based on human harmony and convivial tools. This vision accepts the norms of universal justice of the previous level but redirects them toward the establishment of a new and more just world. For people to grow to this level, two other kinds of skills are indispensable, the interpersonal and the imaginal.

## 2. Interpersonal Skills

Human growth is evidently dependent on the cultivation of interpersonal skills that equip a person to enter into deeply satisfying human relationships. There is a noticeable correlation between a person's expansion of consciousness and a widening of social relationships. The person who remains isolated or habitually cut off from others thereby effectively stunts his or her own growth. In order to increase the radius of the social sphere and also to intensify and deepen already existing relationships, a person must acquire special kinds of skills. The following diagram based on Erikson's work can serve to illustrate this:

Columns B, C and D are particularly appropriate to our present discussion. Column B describes the sphere of significant relationships that gradually widens from the "Maternal Person" or primary care-giver at stage one to "Humankind" at stage eight. The movement goes out from the mother, to the family, to the neighborhood, to school and work until it reaches all humankind. At stage six words like "partners in friendship" and "cooperation" suggest the development of more intense relationships.

Column C contains key words that represent concomitant development or, as Erikson puts it, "related elements of social order." As the child relates to these expanding spheres of interpersonal complexity, his or her mind expands and takes in an ever-widening range of social issues. For example, at stage two, experiencing the relationship to parental persons as providers of guidance and direction, the child is furnished with an experiential base for understanding law and order.

### Diagram 2

| | A<br>Psychosocial<br>Crises | B<br>Radius of Significant<br>Relations | C<br>Related Elements of<br>Social Order | D<br>Psychosocial<br>Modalities | E<br>Psychosexual<br>Stages |
|---|---|---|---|---|---|
| I | Trust vs.<br>Mistrust | Maternal Person | Cosmic Order | To get<br>To give in return | Oral-Respiratory,<br>Sensory-Kinesthetic<br>(Incorporative Modes) |
| II | Autonomy vs.<br>Shame, Doubt | Parental Persons | "Law and Order" | To hold (on)<br>To let (go) | Anal-Urethral<br>Muscular<br>(Retentive-Eliminative) |
| III | Initiative vs.<br>Guilt | Basic Family | Ideal Prototypes | To make (=going after)<br>To "make like"<br>(=playing) | Infantile-Genital<br>Locomotor<br>(Intrusive, Inclusive) |
| IV | Industry vs.<br>Inferiority | "Neighborhood,"<br>School | Technological<br>Elements | To make things<br>(=completing)<br>To make things together | "Latency" |
| V | Identity and<br>Repudiation vs.<br>Identity Diffusion | Peer Groups and<br>Outgroups:<br>Models of Leadership | Ideological<br>Perspectives | To be oneself<br>(or not to be)<br>To share being oneself | Puberty |
| VI | Intimacy and<br>Solidarity vs.<br>Isolation | Partners in friendship<br>sex, competition<br>cooperation | Patterns of<br>Cooperation and<br>Competition | To lose and find<br>oneself in<br>another | Genitality |
| VII | Generativity vs.<br>Self-Absorption | Divided labor and<br>shared household | Currents of<br>Education and Tradition | To make be<br>To take care of | |
| VIII | Integrity vs.<br>Despair | Humankind<br>"My Kind" | Wisdom | To be, through<br>having been<br>To face not being | |

*(Identity and the Life Cycle. Selected Papers by Erik H. Erikson, page 166)*

Column D relates more directly to our present subject of skills, even though some of them listed by Erikson are instrumental or imaginal rather than interpersonal, like "to make things" or "to make like." Still, "to make things together," "to be oneself," "to share being oneself," "to lose and find oneself in another," and "to take care of" are all interpersonal skills, some of which will be enlarged upon later. For the moment suffice it to say that Erikson sees these skills as developmental and necessary for growth. Some of these skills like "to share being myself" apply to most human relationships while others like "to lose and find oneself in another" are reserved for only the most intimate kind of relationships.

The ultimate in one dimension of the interpersonal is the capacity to see the whole human race as one's "in-group." To make this a behavioral reality takes incredible skills and represents a gigantic expansion of consciousness that contrasts sharply with the awareness stage of the young child who sees the self as the center of the universe.

The ultimate in another dimension of the interpersonal is the capacity to enter into intimate human relationships where the "I" of consciousness becomes a "we."

The following diagram spells this out:

## Line A—Expanding Relationships

The top line of the diagram represents the enlarging of significant relationships that normally accompanies personal growth. It describes a person's in-groups, a term that Allport[5] suggests resists precise definition.

It is difficult to define an in-group precisely. Perhaps the best that can be done is to say that members of an in-group all use the term *we* with the same essential significance.

This "we" includes more and more people as a person grows.

The way we view our in-groups identifies our basic loyalties. These loyalties quite literally permit us to see where "we're at" because they clarify identity by bringing into focus where we see ourselves belonging. In this regard Allport writes:

Thus the sense of belonging is a highly personal matter. Even two members of the same actual in-group may view its composition in widely divergent ways. Take for instance the definition that two Americans might give to their own national in-group.

| native white Protestant gentiles | native white Protestant gentiles, Negroes, Catholics, Jews, Immigrants, Etc. |
|---|---|
| as seen by individual A | as seen by individual B |

**Fig. 1.**
**The national in-group as perceived by two Americans.**

The narrowed perception of individual A is the product of an arbitrary categorization, one that he or she finds convenient (functionally significant) to hold. The larger range of perception on the part of the individual B creates a wholly different conception of the national in-group. It is misleading to say that both belong to the same in-group. Psychologically they do not.

Normally an in-group implies an out-group, hostility toward which tends to increase one's in-group loyalties. But this need not be so. A person reaching Phase IV sees humankind as the in-group, leaving nobody on the outside. Admittedly when a person accepts such

## Diagram 3

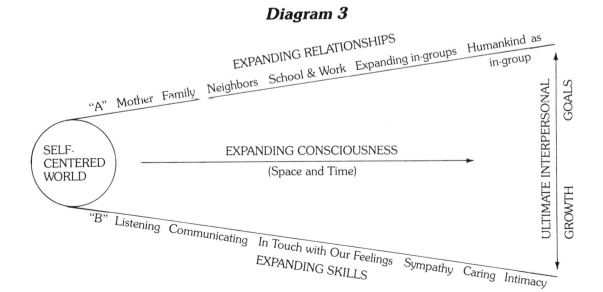

an all-encompassing in-group, intense and warm loyalty is difficult to generate. It calls for attaining as a behavioral reality the kind of lofty ideals that typify visionaries like Jesus (love your enemies).

## Line B—Expanding Skills

Line B in Diagram 3 lists some of the skills that must be acquired if relating to any in-group is to be meaning-enhancing. In this regard the intimate relationship can function as a prism that breaks down and makes possible the identification of the various skills that enter into the developing and sustaining of human relationships.

An intimate relationship is one in which I share my innermost being, my hopes and fears, anxieties and aspirations, my thoughts and emotions with another human being in such a way that I encourage him or her to feel free to do likewise.

Obviously such a relationship is beyond the grasp of any persons who can neither attentively listen to another nor accurately communicate their own thoughts and feelings. These skills basic to any human relationship must be fostered at home and early in a child's school experience.

A most essential interpersonal skill and yet one often neglected is the ability to get in touch with one's own feelings. Most people learn to express what they think about something, for example about their mistreatment by somebody. But how many people in the face of mistreatment are able to sort out and deal maturely with how they feel about such an experience? Until one can do this, one does not really know one's innermost being and therefore cannot share that inner self with another.

Empathy is the ability to get in touch with the feelings of another. As Thomas Oden says in *Game Free:*

Empathy is the capacity for one person to enter imaginatively into the sphere of consciousness of another, to feel the specific contours of another's experience, to allow one's imagination to risk entering the inner experiencing process of another.[6]

Persons who develop this skill can sustain many friendships; without it intimacy is impossible.

Oden builds his discussion of intimacy around six antitheses that he finally breaks down into the following negatively stated points:

1. Intimate relationships do not grow if not given time.
2. Intimate bonding is less palpable if it never has ways of becoming intensified into ecstatic moments of intimate sharing.
3. If relationships lack contractual clarity or if the contracts are easily terminable, then to that degree the relationship is less intimate-capable.

4. If within the framework of sustained accountability the relationship is not able to be renegotiated in the light of specific new demands and occasions, then it is less likely to be intimate.
5. If partners are unable to empathize with each other's feelings, intimacy is inhibited.
6. If partners are unable to feel their own feelings clearly and fully, then the empathy that intimacy requires is constricted.
7. If emotive warmth is absent consistently, one is not likely to call the relationship intimate.
8. Relationships that are unable to face conflicts are less likely to develop intimacy.
9. Insofar as partners need to resort to deceptive and manipulative behaviors or lack honest self-disclosure, the relationship is to that degree probably less intimate.
10. To the extent that the relationship requires the constant monitoring of one party and thus inhibits the self-direction of the other, intimacy is decreased.
11. Insofar as the relationship is not recognized as finite and therefore vulnerable to death, it is less likely to achieve genuine intimacy because it will be prone to idolize the partner.

Described in that rather extended quote are the kinds of interpersonal skills that must be acquired if the growth goal of intimacy is to become a real possibility.

Following are two diagrams that further clarify this area of interpersonal relationships. Diagram 4 is simply an elaboration of line A from Diagram 3 that attempts to spell out how one at each phase would decide who is a member of one's in-group and who must be consigned to the out-group. The middle column merely indicates the bonds that might unite people of each phase of consciousness. Diagram 5 presents a breakdown of six important interpersonal skills.

## 3. Imaginal Skills

In actuality a fertile imagination is an indispensable element in the acquisition and exercise of all the skills already considered. It takes imagination to design tools or to relate creatively to other persons. Still we have not yet explicitly investigated the structure and role of the human imagination.

Both Wugga and Chug serve as excellent models of persons with great imaginative resources. When the natural environment with its cold and its rain turned on them, Chug did not passively submit to its power, but by creative use of his imagination he figured out how to start a fire. When Wugga felt the need to gath-

## Diagram 4

### A Developmental View of Significant Others

| | IN-GROUP | BOND | OUT-GROUP |
|---|---|---|---|
| **P H A S E I** | —I<br><br>—I and those on my side who help me get my way | —Tyranny of my ego<br><br>—My self-centered needs and interests | —My competitors for security and pleasure<br><br>—Those who oppose me in my efforts to get my own way |
| **P H A S E II** | —I and the "they" who count—family, peers<br><br>—The establishment and its supporters | —Attraction to those like myself<br><br>—My need for approval<br><br>—Strong reliance on authority conceived autocratically | —Those who do not count or oppose those who do<br><br>—Those who oppose the establishment |
| **P H A S E III** | —I and those who share my causes<br><br>—I and others who are evaluating the establishment | —Ideals and objectives of my causes<br><br>—Common concern about opponents and the establishment<br><br>—Democratic type of authority | —Opponents of my causes<br><br>—Conformists<br><br>—Rigid Institutionalism |
| **P H A S E IV** | —We who are building a new world<br><br>—Humanity<br><br>—The created order | —Vision of new world<br><br>—Relatedness based on interdependence<br><br>—Authority—shared responsibility | —Opponents of harmony<br><br>—No out-group |

er more food than her two hands could carry, she made the imaginative leap to the notion of a container, and using the resources in the environment, she invented a basket.

When faced with predatory intentions of their neighbors, Chug did not despair but used his imagination and powers of persuasion to come up with an alternative to the seemingly inevitable loss of their house. This is the use of the imagination to create hopeful alternatives.

Their responsibilities on the community council repeatedly taxed Wugga's and Chug's imaginative resources. In the face of numerous new and challenging problems confronting them in building a complex human organization, they had to originate human institutions that would appropriately answer those challenges. Here they used imagination to create tools that would modify human beings. In this instance, Chug and Wugga benefited from the assistance of oth-

er citizens of Chuwuggatown, making this a communal as well as a personal use of the imagination.

## THE STRUCTURE OF THE IMAGINATION

What we mean by the imagination is the synergetic interaction between the fantasy, the emotions and the reflective intellect of human beings. This process of interaction results in a product, the idea, which is a miniaturization of data that has been gathered from the person's environment, evaluated, organized and reflected on constructively. What does all this mean?

First of all, one must recognize that the imagination is not three things but an integrated whole here divided into three components only for the purpose of clearly identifying three different aspects of the imagination's activity.

*Fantasy* refers to the operation of the imagination that uses psychic energy to convert data received from

23

## Diagram 5

### Some Interpersonal Skills

| SKILL | SOME COMPONENTS | SOME OBSTACLES |
|---|---|---|
| General Communication | Ability to verbalize<br><br>Sense of self-worth—confidence<br><br>Imagination<br>Spontaneity<br>Enjoyment of others<br>Accuracy and precision | Lack of verbal skills<br><br>Self-consciousness—lack of confidence<br><br>Lack of trust of others<br>Lack of imagination<br>Fear of disapproval |
| Listening | Attentiveness to another<br><br>Curiosity<br><br>Expanding interests<br><br>Ability to concentrate | Excessive preoccupation, with self<br>Indifference to others<br><br>Physical orientation—too body conscious<br>Lack of self control |
| In Touch With My Own Feelings | Ability to listen to emotions<br><br>Appreciation of emotions as valuable sources of information and as life enrichers<br><br>Ability to constructively use emotions as judgment faculty | Suppression of emotions<br><br>Ignoring emotions<br><br>Fearing emotions<br>Inability to use emotions constructively<br><br>Inaccurate interpretations of one's feelings |
| Empathy | Sensitivity to feelings of another<br><br>Ability to identify with another<br><br>Lively imagination<br><br>Objective mental attitude<br><br>Intuition | Indifference toward others<br><br>Preoccupation with "D" needs<br><br>Overly subjective mental attitude<br><br>Lack of imagination |
| Caring | Openness and availability<br>Empathy<br>Happy with self<br>Willingness to let others be themselves<br>Pain tolerance | "D" need orientation<br>Need to control others<br>Too busy with self<br>Lack of empathy |
| Intimacy | Tolerance for self-disclosure<br>Willing to be accountable for another<br>Conflict capability<br><br>Emotional Warmth<br>Consistency | Secretive about self<br><br>Inconsistency or fickleness<br><br>Intolerant of demands of others<br><br>Intolerant of Conflict |

either external or internal (the memory or the unconscious) sources into images consisting of colors, shapes, sounds, and movement. This image-making ability while natural to all humans is more developed in some people than in others. For example, accomplished artists are capable of elaborating complex images that they in turn imprint on canvas, stone or wood.

As she contemplated the problem of how to transport large quantities of food, Wugga was able to create an internal image of a container that she later externalized (objectified). Her internal process of considering the elements of the problem, i.e., the distance, the need to carry the baby, issued in a product, first the idea, then the basket itself. The complex data were simplified or miniaturized into a single idea—basket.

*The emotions* in this context designate a person's feeling-response to the data picked up from the environment. The emotions evaluate the data, perceiving it as helpful or harmful, desirable or to be avoided. We have good and bad feelings about things. It is rare that data are neutral. Shapes and colors and sounds may in themselves be neutral, but normally they are present in images as qualifiers of something else that does have emotional significance. Sometimes images from a person's unconscious even enter consciousness with emotional overtones that are not comprehended.

Thus there is interaction between the fantasy and the emotions. The emotions evaluate and pass judgment on the images created by the fantasy. Chug's internal image of cold and rain and physical discomfort was evaluated by the emotions as unpleasant. It was the activity of the reflective intellect that supplied the fantasy with new data leading to the formation of new images, such as a fire burning in the cave, which in turn called for new evaluations—the cave as pleasant and warm.

## Diagram 6

| THE DATA | THE PROCESS | THE PROCESS |
|---|---|---|
| ENVIRONMENTAL DATA<br><br>COLD AND RAIN | FANTASY<br><br>IMAGE OF COLD AND RAIN . . .<br><br>LATER OF WARM HOUSE<br>EMOTIONS—<br>Uncomfortable and Anxious, Later happy with House<br>REFLECTIVE INTELLECT —<br>Considering How to deal with weather, i.e. alternatives | THE IDEA<br>Wugga's Internal Response—<br>An Idea of A House<br><br>EXTERNALIZED INTO |

| Wugga and Chug in RAIN AND COLD | Wugga in CAVE USING IMAGINATION | Wugga and Chug's HOUSE |
|---|---|---|

*The reflective intellect* examines and organizes the data picked up from the environment (as depicted by the fantasy and judged by the emotions) with a view to simplifying the data and constructing an idea (miniaturization). One of the key activities of the reflective intellect so typical of creative people is to conjure up and consider alternative ways of dealing with data. This explains why the imagination is so often described as the faculty that enables a person to see alternatives to reality as presently constituted.

It was this kind of activity that allowed Wugga to construct a basket and a clay pot and to weave together vines and saplings to make a shelter. A less imaginative person than Chug, when faced by a band of hostile cavedwellers might have felt trapped or doomed. However, Chug not only originated a creative alternative for his group, but convinced his would-be foes that this alternative could also benefit them. That took imagination.

So these are the three operations that characterize the activity of the active imagination. But the imagination does more than produce simple ideas. It also combines several ideas so as to form a hypothesis and then uses the hypothesis to examine new data to form a theory. Eventually after sufficient testing of the theory, it may formulate a law like Newton's law of gravity.

*Miniaturization* is operative in all the activities contained in the above diagram. All are examples of complexity being simplified or compressed. The idea is a miniaturization of external data. The hypothesis is the miniaturization of several ideas; the hypothesis and new data result in a theory that with the test of time may become a law.

Through the imaginal skills human beings modify their external environment by applying ideas in creative (and unfortunately also in destructive) tool making. The imaginal skills apply equally to tools that modify the physical environment (Wugga's basket), tools that modify human beings (the human institutions that regulated life in Chuwuggatown) and tools that enhance life (works of fine art).

# IMAGINATION AND SELF-ACTUALIZATION

In any one of the three operations of the imagination discussed above, persons may either hinder or promote their own development. Stated another way, how we use our imaginations plays a large role in determining where we are developmentally.

As we interact with the environment, it is imagination that determines whether we will be responders or creators.

If, for whatever reasons, we adopt a generally passive attitude toward the environment, we will not demonstrate the creativity characteristic of an imaginative person. Such individuals are responsive rather than original, content to let others take the initiative and then to shape their own activity into a reply to the demands originating in an environment largely controlled by others.

# EDUCATORS AND IMAGINAL SKILLS

In order for the imagination to be stimulated, basic needs (Phase I and II needs), security, approval and a sense of personal adequacy and worth have to be minimally satisfied. At this point a person can begin to explore alternatives to his or her present lifestyle. But imagination must be stimulated by teachers, educators, leaders—those one looks up to.

## Stunting Imaginal Growth

It is not difficult to imagine the kind of home and school environments that might discourage imaginal growth. Following is a list of some possible environmental factors that would inhibit the development of the imagination:

1. Presence of the style of authority that creates dependency.
2. Discouragement and even punishment of initiative.
3. Fatalistic approach to life—"whatever will be will be."
4. An absence of challenges that stretch the resources of family members.
5. Success so stressed that fear of failure is strong and initiative and experimentation discouraged.
6. An absence of a creative use of leisure, for example, poetry, fairy tales, family dreaming, travel, knowledge of other cultures.

## Fostering Imaginal Growth

Among the characteristics of an environment that can encourage the imagination are the following:

1. Authority is democratic in style, encourages initiative.
2. There is enough consistency in daily life to support security, but pliability and variety have their place.
3. Members are given challenges that stretch their resources but in a supportive fashion that is not too demanding.
4. Resourcefulness and experimentation, even if they lead to failure, are rewarded.
5. There is creative use of leisure, family reading, travel, varied vacation patterns, familiarity with other cultures, past and present.
6. Group problem solving (brainstorming) is a frequent experience.

7. Honest self-expression and independence are valued.

## Imaginal Skills and Valuing

Valuing as a process is itself an imaginal skill. For it is only possible for one to choose from alternatives after considering the consequences to the extent that one has an active imagination. However, imaginal activity that is not based soundly on limitations—indeed, the consciousness of the limitations of my entire reality—is an unreal and non-productive exercise in dreaming.

In short, imaginal skills if they are to be balanced and healthy must include the following:

1. The ability to fantasize and create new alternatives.
2. The ability to see another's reality and see its alternatives.
3. The ability to see the consequences of the alternatives (negative as well as positive) and to prioritize the more productive ones.
4. The ability to criticize and evaluate situations and read their potential and limitations.
5. The ability to be able to project concrete practical (constructive) suggestions from the imagined alternatives (tool making).

Quite concretely imaginal skills relate to all the other skills as shown in *Diagram 7*.

# 4. System Skills

System skills enable one to see the parts in relation to the whole. They include the ability to analyze a complex whole into its parts, to grasp the inter-relationships among the parts, to plan interventions to change existing systems, and to design new systems. Clearly, system skills depend upon the development and integration of the other three sets of skills, and therefore are the last to be developed.

There are at least three basic kinds of systems with which a person must learn to deal:

1. One's own body
2. One's family
3. Societal institutions

## THE BODY AS SYSTEM

Unless we possess skills in managing our own bodies, effort expended in gaining other systems skills will be largely wasted. The body is a complicated and powerful system whose demands are delivered without any prior consultation and often without prior warning. To ignore or lack the skills to respond appropriately to those demands is to risk and even to encourage being controlled by the body. No existing form of governing devised by human beings operates as autocratically as the human body.

## Diagram 7

| Imaginal | Instrumental | Interpersonal | Systems |
|---|---|---|---|
| Fantasy Creating new alternatives | New abilities widen alternatives | Meeting new people widens one's possibilities | Systems make alternatives possible through human cooperation |
| Seeing another's alternatives | All cognitive learning increases alternatives through increased Ideas | To the extent I see another's ideas and possibilities mine are increased | Analysis of systems leads to alternative ways of renewing institutions |
| Seeing consequences and creatively prioritizing | Technology can help us foresee outcomes | Experiences of love and intimacy change my priorities | Systems modeling is a way of creating viable futures and avoiding some negative consequences |
| Criticizing and evaluating | Evaluation and statistical analysis are developed instrumental tools | Viewing my limitations through healthy criticism enables me to evaluate my potential realistically | Evaluating systems is a step toward creating alternatives and freeing imaginal skills to work |
| Making concrete suggestions (tools) | Tool making is an instrumental skill | Interpersonal skills are human tools | A system is a human tool |

Therefore persons interested in their own growth must develop health skills in caring for their bodies. The ability of Wugga and Chug to complete the many projects to which they devoted themselves was clearly dependent on their bodily health. Had they not headed for the cave to escape the chilling rain, they might quite possibly have died from pneumonia.

## HEALTH: BEING ONE'S OWN DOCTOR

The primary responsibility for health care belongs to oneself. Far too many people see their health as being in the hands of their doctor in much the same way as they see the smooth running of their automobiles as a matter for their garage mechanic. Of course there are times when the special expertise of physicians is needed, but one should not abdicate one's primary responsibility in this area. The role of the physician is to assist individuals in the exercise of responsibility for their own health. The more knowledge and skill individuals acquire, the less often will a doctor's assistance be needed.

Ultimately, fitness is a matter of maintaining a harmonious balance between the individual and the environment, and between the various forces at work in the human body. Health is a systems problem, a problem of dealing with the complexities of ever-changing external and internal environments and with the relations between them. Under the conditions of modern life, the external environment bombards us with noise, air pollution, exposure to dangerous chemicals and radiation, overcrowding, abundant and confusing alternatives, the pressures of competition. Moreover, we often attempt to reduce the resultant strains by voluntarily taking additional stressors into our systems in the form of excess foods, tobacco, alcohol and drugs.

We may not be able to do a great deal about the external environment, except perhaps to remove ourselves to a less polluted area or to a less stressful work situation, but as the concept of stress management suggests, we can acquire the skills to manage our daily lives for optimum health and vitality. A human being is a complex system—physical, mental, emotional—with wonderful powers of adaptation, self-healing and self-renewal. A person must learn to listen to the body's demands, to be aware of one's feelings, and to judge what response is consistent with over-all harmony. A migraine headache or an upset stomach may signal the need for a change in one's over-all pattern of living. Modern Americans tend to think of health and disease in terms of specific remedies for specific problems: a pain killer for the headache, a diuretic for high blood pressure, perhaps even surgery to remove an ulcerated section of the stomach. But at best these are temporary expedients. A long-term cure depends on better management of one's entire system. The basic skills here include building up one's physical fitness through proper nutrition, rest and exercise, restricting or eliminating one's intake of such stressors as alcohol, reducing anxiety and fostering peace of mind through life goal setting, financial planning, learning basic techniques of relaxation and meditation, and developing a well-integrated personal support system among one's intimates, friends and colleagues.

It is significant that although modern medicine has made enormous strides in the control of infectious diseases—smallpox, yellow fever, malaria—we face a rapid increase in the stress-induced disorders: high blood pressure, heart disease, ulcers, cancer, mental illness. The holistic health movements suggest that the remedies for these conditions are to be found not so much in new medications but rather in developing a better balanced pattern of living: healthier rhythms of work and leisure, rest and exercise, solitude and intimacy. Helpful methods include both the ancient disciplines of yoga and Zen and the modern methods of psychosynthesis (developed by Robert Assagioli) and bio-feedback. Such methods teach bodily relaxation and reduction of anxiety and help the person to shield the self from the pressures of the surrounding world.

The ability to deal with one's body and one's total self to maintain health is the most basic systems skill needed by every human being.

## THE FAMILY AS SYSTEM

The first system outside of one's own body with which a child must learn to cope is the family. The child is so constituted that as it moves from a comfortable intrauterine existence where the needs for nourishment and warmth have been automatically met, it is forced to direct attention outward to the external environment in order to discover new ways of satisfying basic needs. This shift produces the first major expansion of consciousness and, like all later development, is need-related. In this new environment, the mother or other primary care giver is the key figure.

While in the process of becoming familiar with his or her new world, the child acquires the ability to manipulate mother so as to have her take care of the needs for food, warmth and physical comfort. It learns that crying, whether in anger or in discomfort, frequently evokes the desired response from mother. The language of reward and punishment is the only one that the small child can understand. That same language enables the child to discover not only what to expect from others but also what others expect from him or her. In learning to get along in the family, the child develops an awareness of the expectations of significant others—mother, father, siblings, perhaps even a grandparent or an aunt or uncle. Through repeated experimentation, the child settles into a more or less consistent approach to the family.

It is within the family environment that the child gains the conviction that he or she has a place in the world and that the world is safe and fairly predictable. Such a conviction provides the child with an embryonic sense of belonging that must eventually deepen if the individual is ever to mature.

In this regard, speaking of disadvantaged families, Salvador Minuchin in *Families of the Slums* writes:

One essential feature of the family and home environment is its impermanence and unpredictability. These characteristics make it difficult for the growing child to define himself in relation to his world. In home visits we encountered a world in which objects and events have a transient quality. For example, a bed shared by two or more children can be turned over to a different child or to a semi-permanent visitor while its original occupants are crowded into a section of another bed. The geography of the home and its arrangements impede the development of a sense that "I have my place in the world."[7]

In such an environment it is difficult to imagine how a child's basic needs for security, pleasure, belonging and self-worth can be satisfied. Such children will inevitably learn the skills to meet these basic human demands. But their world views will tend to remain at an earlier phase because of the physical environment and the way they have to adapt to the environment, given their limited experience and lack of resourcefulness. A person trying to help such children must use as much effort in attempting to create a more healthy environment as in ministering to the psychic needs of the children. The two elements are interrelated.

Virginia Satir mentions the following skill-related lessons that parents must give their children if healthy growth is to take place.

1. To teach "roles" or socially accepted ways to act with others in different social situations. (These roles vary according to the age and sex of the child.)
2. To teach the child to cope with the inanimate environment.
3. To teach the child how to communicate, how to use words and gestures so that they will have a generally accepted meaning for others.
4. To teach how and when to express emotions, generally guiding the child's emotional reactivity. (The family teaches the child by appealing to love and to fear, communicating verbally, non-verbally, and by example.)[8]

These are merely some of the skills with which children must equip themselves if they are to deal effectively with the family and later with the larger human community. In terms of learning to cope with that larger world out there, Satir maintains that it is especially important that the child, within the family, develop esteem for self, both as a capable person and as a sexual person. The parents have the responsibility for providing the type of family environment that reinforces values such as self-esteem, womanhood, or manhood.

While these interpersonal coping skills are important for harmonious living in the family and for subsequent personal development, they still fall short of true systems skills. The key is in understanding the family as a complex whole, whose members are both unique individuals and interdependent actors, affecting each other in somewhat the same way that the various parts of the body do. Family counselors have given us many insights into the family as a system. They learned long ago that individual treatment of an emotionally disturbed child in a family may be totally fruitless, for the child may be ill as a consequence of interactions in the total system. For instance, if the mother and father are continually fighting over the father's gambling habits, the child may not get enough attention. The sickness may be an adaptation to that situation, a device for getting attention. The child has learned a coping strategy, but one which is not particularly healthy and which may not work in other systems, such as the school or the work place. Treating the child alone may effect temporary improvement, but soon the pattern will repeat itself unless the therapist through understanding how the family members are relating to each other, that is, through systems skills, is able to help them change the pattern of their relationships.

Similarly, the women's movement has increased our insights into the family as system. The consciousness-raising groups that were particularly prominent in the early years of the movement represented for innumerable women the step from coping skills to systems skills. They moved from a sense of personal guilt and failure in an unsatisfactory marriage to an understanding of the family as a system, the conflicting role expectations it places on women, the constricting definitions of women's roles, and the underlying patriarchal ideology that legitimates economic and legal discrimination. In the light of these insights, individual women were able to reconstruct family patterns, step into new roles in the work place and in the political arena, and organize to effect changes in the legal, credit and other systems.

## SOCIAL INSTITUTIONS OF VARYING COMPLEXITY

As we grow through the phases of consciousness, our world expands and we find ourselves confronted with more and more systems. The children grow up and have to go to school where they must deal with schoolmates, teachers and administrators. Eventually we go to work where we must meet the expectations of a boss and of co-workers. The systems get more complicated and demand more ingenuity from a person than the family ever did.

Wugga and Chug demonstrated their systems skills when they organized their cohorts to learn and practice the new skills they had discovered. They had the foresight to recognize what needs might arise in their newly founded town and also possessed the ability to plan and organize the people to meet those needs.

The successful revolutionary offers an example of fantastic systems skills. He must be able to read the expectations of the masses. (Hitler was a master at this.) He must have a sense of timing and an ability to foresee obstacles. And of course without the gifts to excite the imagination of his followers, he could never get the revolution off the ground. Throughout the whole revolutionary process, he must organize people, distribute tasks and adapt to the unexpected. Lenin, Castro and Chairman Mao have all exhibited these qualities. Those who have organized movements for social change in the United States—Elizabeth Cady Stanton, Carrie Chapman Catt, John L. Lewis, Martin Luther King, Jr., Betty Friedan, Ralph Nader, to name a few—have demonstrated high level systems skills.

The observations made thus far might lead one to conclude that systems skills are to be cultivated only by the leaders of an organization. But anyone who is affected by a system must learn to deal with it. Just as the child has to learn to define a role within the family

and live with it, so must any individual define a role in the more complex systems in which we live today. Moreover, as we learn to deal with a given system, we may forge new roles for ourselves and even intervene to make changes in the system. These too are needed skills.

## INTEGRATION AS SKILL

The model shown in Diagram 8 may help us to see the units of body, family and larger institutions as systems.

All three systems are similar. As system they *all* have similar tensions:

*Need-Tasks*—The tension is between the individual's needs and the system's own goals, values or tasks. In the body as system an individual may want to work all night to get the job done, *but* the body as a system might not be able to take it—it has its own peculiar rules and limits. An individual in a family might want everyone to go out to a picnic on Sunday, but the family may have prior commitments to visit relatives—as a whole family.

In Diagram 8 reducing the tension between personal needs and the task of the institution is the perennial job of the manager and leader. The task might be profit versus minimal security for the employee.

## SOME SYSTEM SKILLS

It is difficult, if not impossible, to formulate a complete breakdown of the skills needed to cope with complex systems. But certainly some of the more important skills needed are the following:

### Diagram 8

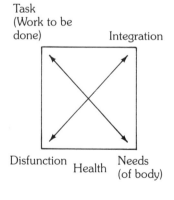

Task (Work to be done) — Integration
Disfunction — Health — Needs (of body)

**Body**

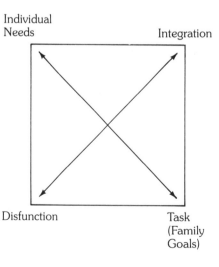

Individual Needs — Integration
Disfunction — Task (Family Goals)

**Family**

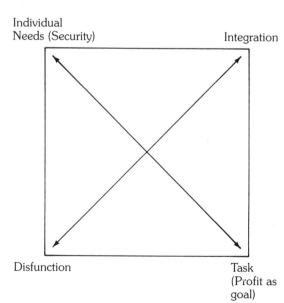

Individual Needs (Security) — Integration
Disfunction — Task (Profit as goal)

**Institution**

1. The ability to read the present and future expectations of the system as represented by the leadership or the membership.

2. The ability to discover or shape a personal role in the fulfillment of those expectations by making sure the system wants and needs me.

3. The ability to foresee and handle obstacles and opposition.

4. The ability to read the signs of the time as they are significant for both me and the system.

5. The ability to motivate myself and others to achieve the goals of the system.

6. The ability to analyze the components of a task and to make sure that each is taken care of, assigning specific responsibilities in the process.

7. The ability to assess both the strong and weak points of the system.

8. The ability to decide on realistic goals for the system.

9. The ability to enhance personal meaning from my being part of the system.

10. The ability to distinguish between the myth and the reality of the system, to separate propaganda from reality.

## SYSTEMS SKILLS AND DEVELOPMENT

An added point to bear in mind is that what is a skill at one stage of a person's development might become an impediment to growth at a later stage. For example, as one moves out beyond the family into society, initially one needs to learn to fit into that society and its systems. But if the basic concern as one involves oneself in these systems is only to conform or fit in, then growth to Phase III will be prevented by the unwillingness to become self-directed. What was a valuable skill and means for achieving a sense of belonging at one time has now become a liability. Passive responses should eventually give way to creative initiative and active responsibility.

In the same vein unless manipulative behavior that is normal and necessary in the young child is replaced by an ability to evoke free and genuine responses from other people, maturity will remain permanently out of reach. Recently I have been counseling a twenty-three-year-old male who has an aversion to getting a job. Married and father of a son, he has thus far managed to get by through manipulating others—his mother, his wife and his in-laws—so that they meet his financial responsibilities. Manipulation has worked for him so well for so long that it seems never to have occurred to him that other approaches might ultimately be more satisfying. His systems skills are destructive rather than creative toward others. He has recently discovered that complex systems like finance companies

and others typical of the working world do not respond favorably to his manipulative efforts which are actually directed at avoiding responsibility and its hardships.

So skills appropriate to one stage of development need to be discarded and replaced by others more consistent with the next stage of development. Normally, people integrate their behavior to fit the results they desire. As they develop to later phases, their skills are geared to cooperative accomplishment rather than personal needs only.

## LEADERSHIP

The leadership in any system has to have the maturity to recognize that their responsibility is to do more than keep order or make people comfortable. They must not confuse care for the members of the system with refusal to cause confrontation and conflict where that is necessary. They are integrators of tension within limits. They must have real vision if they are to move people to higher levels of maturity. In this and other areas of systems behavior, moral issues become prominent.

A moral issue arises because systems have a way of accentuating and reinforcing the powerlessness of individuals. Systems sometimes tend to crush the individual and take control of his or her life. This not only inhibits growth but it destroys a person's individuality. Every system needs people with vision skilled in integrative or change processes who can bring such abuses to consciousness and pave the way for reform.

Morality is also involved when the leadership tolerates all manner of corruption and abuses of responsibility that poison the whole system. Again there is a need to build into the system strong communication networks which can serve as watchdogs.

These are merely some of the systems skills that are essential to growth. At present there seems to be very little thought or energy devoted to the development of these kinds of skills in our educational institutions.

---

## *Skill and Development*

---

We now need to take a look at some concrete examples of the relationship between the development of values and the acquisition of the four skills.

We will use Diagram 9 as a reference point as we discuss the following examples. First let us look at Case 1.

### A Hospital Administrator

Rosemary was an administrator of a 1,500-bed hospital in a large city. She was experiencing loneliness and doubts about her self-worth due to the fact that she was approaching retirement and had very few friends. She also felt that her role as administrator in the hospital being one of authority did not permit her to get to know people in her work situation very well. During a consultation session we asked Rosemary, utilizing pictures from magazines, to construct a collage on how she saw herself and her life vocation.

To make the story brief, once she had described her picture we were able to pull out underlying values that she said were representative of her own behavioral priorities. She listed them as follows: (1) self-competence, (2) achievement, (3) independence, (4) self-worth. As she described this ranking she noted that self-worth was very important to her and was low on her list because of her sense of loneliness, even though she had gained a great deal of self-worth through her ability to achieve and through her recognized competence in the medical field. However, she also said that a high priority for her was independence, but it was third on the list because running the hospital, which was the most important thing to her, made independent action difficult. When she was asked how she would like these values to be prioritized in her behavior, she ranked them as follows: (1) self-worth, (2) independence, (3) self-competence and (4) achievement. Interestingly she described independence as being able to do some creative things on her own and get to know new people.

She felt that self-worth meant much to her because she was lonely and would like to have something in her life other than work. As we began looking at the situation we recognized that in her initial ranking that described her behavior the first two values are from the second phase of consciousness and the third one is at the third phase. When she described how she would like to be, the value that came from the third phase of consciousness moved to first place. Reflecting on this situation we might conclude that we have here a description of a person growing from one phase of development to another.

As she described herself she noted that she had a high sense of competence and was in fact able to achieve and deal with the system of the hospital effectively. One would therefore assume that she would naturally move into that third phase of development. But as she herself noted there was something that stopped her. An obvious conclusion was that it might have something to do with self-worth.

It is at this point that we recognize that a confluent theory of values does not help at all if it only helps us to describe the values that are present. This is the role of value clarification, which only describes "what is"

### Diagram 9
### VALUES AND MORAL DEVELOPMENT

|  | WORLD VIEW | VALUES | MORAL DEVELOPMENT |
|---|---|---|---|
| P H A S E I | World as Mystery *(Pre-Conventional-Physical) Self as Center | Survival Security Pleasure Wonder | *Survival: Avoidance of Pain Self-Happiness |
| P H A S E II | World as Problem *(Conventional—Social) Self as Belonging | Belonging Work Self Competence Self Worth | *Peer Image: "Good Girl/ Boy Orientation" Authority is right by virtue of office |
| P H A S E III | World as Project and Invention *(Post Conventional—Conscience) Self as Independent | Independence Fairness for all Service Creativity | *Law Order Orientation— Evaluated and change within Innate Intuitive Conscience, Justice |
| P H A S E IV | World as Mystery Cared For (Contemvenutal—Congruent) Selves as Life Givers | Harmony Interdependence Intimacy Synergy | Orientation Toward Interdependence, Wholeness and Intimacy Orientation Toward action based on a convivial awareness— whole system orientation |

The Four Skills Needed for Integrated Development:
(1) Instrumental skills (2) Interpersonal skills (3) Imaginal skills (4) System skills

*Cf. L. Kohlberg

and does not help a person to move anywhere but only takes, so to speak, a photographic shot of a moment, helping people see where they are.

In order to see the developmental picture more clearly we need to look at the four sets of skills. When Rosemary described her four skills, she noted that she had done very well in both systems and instrumental skills but felt that she was not a very creative person and often had difficulty in relating to people. This made it evident that a lack of interpersonal skills contributed to her diminished sense of self-worth. A program of development for her would have to help her structure her personal relationships or obtain assistance in relating better to people so that her self-worth could be enhanced, and this would in fact allow her to grow into another phase of development. In short she needed to develop interpersonal skills.

As we looked into her history we found a woman who really knew a great deal about the workings of the hospital, had no difficulty in talking to persons in authority, and was able to raise money and get things done efficiently. In short she had good instrumental and systems skills. Then, as is often the case, the system responded to her systems skills and made her administrator of the hospital. But leadership that is interdependent and holistic requires more than instrumental and basic systems skills.

For example, without imaginal skills a leader would not be able to move the system along but would simply end by maintaining what had been. It is imagination that enables the leader to have vision. As we investigated, we found that this was the case with Rosemary. Then too because of her lack of interpersonal skills, she tended to move the system along with a blatant disregard for the people involved. She did not dislike people; on the contrary she simply lacked sufficient interpersonal skills.

## Leadership

The last example points to the minimal requirements that are necessary for a person in a leadership position. Obviously the person who is placed at the head of an organization can no longer be dependent on others but rather has to plan and initiate. In terms of phases of development, this must mean that the person is *minimally* at the third phase of consciousness with the needed *concomitant* skills. Contemporary society requires at least that much.

The televised Watergate hearings presented many instances of leaders who had not achieved an ability to make independent judgments consistent with the third phase. The classic example was when ex-Attorney General Mitchell was asked by the Watergate committee why it was that he had not recognized that he had done anything wrong. Mitchell replied, "I put my trust in the role of the president." Looking back to Diagram 9, we note that Mitchell's response was at the the second phase of development, the image orientation that views external authority as right by virtue of its office. The Watergate committee however came at him from a level where innate intuitive judgments of conscience were expected of him as a minimal leadership requirement. As Kohlberg's research has indicated, when persons are separated by more than one level there is little communication. If any of you watched the hearings you would recognize that Mitchell and the Watergate committee passed like ships in the night—there was no communication.

The goal of effective leadership training should at least be the third phase. To return to Rosemary, we simply are asserting that in order to be holistically present at that phase as a leader one has to have all four skills operating in one's behavior at that phase. The person must be able to move the organization with vision (systems and imaginal skills) and yet be able to deal with individuals in a caring manner (interpersonal skills). At the same time he or she must be able to deal with the system and must have the professional skills to pull it off (instrumental and systems skills).

Rosemary's difficulty was that she had only two of the skills at a sufficiently high phase. This presented problems not only because she could not manage the organization in a comfortable way, but also because her own individual development as a human being was being frustrated. So it is necessary for leadership to have all these skills. Moreover, it is necessary for an institution to insist that leadership have all these skills, for only in this way will environments be reinforced that will help individuals grow rather than be locked into a static level of moral development. Institutions need to encourage the kind of leadership that is integrated, holistic and ethical in its development.

Clearly then a confluent theory of values must take into consideration the four skills as well as the total developmental process.

## Interpersonal Skills Revisited

Another short example can serve to make us aware of the need for acquiring all four skills. Recently there has been a great emphasis in psychological literature on interpersonal skills as being essential to integrated development. However it seems to us a mistake to assume in an unqualified way that the interpersonal skills are the most important. This emphasis has more to do with the fact that persons holding this opinion are often at the beginning of the third phase of development and therefore stress honesty and communication as if little else mattered. In fact interpersonal skills would probably be ranked first among the four skills for a person at that third phase of development. Our opinion is that different skills assume priority depending on the stage of development of the individual even within a particular phase of consciousness.

For example we have come across many cases where an individual has excellent imaginal, instrumental and interpersonal skills. Often such a person has gone a long way in an organization as a consequence and has been promoted into a leadership position on the basis of the ability to get along well with people.

What happens, however, is that the person will then be promoted to a position of leadership that is reinforcing him or her to be at that third phase of consciousness at a time when he or she does not have sufficient systems skills.

As a consequence the person then approaches systems interpersonally because the interpersonal skills are the only ones available for dealing with people. But then such a person is more often than not seen as a manipulator of others. Such a person will get into a business meeting and play on emotions to obtain the desired results from the meeting. This, of course, causes alienation and inhibits personal growth.

The point here is that in helping such a person in leadership training, one would not simply brand the person as a manipulator but rather would point out that the problem is a lack of integration and highlight the need for more systems skills. Such systems skills can be acquired through management courses. The point is that at each level a person needs a new set of skills.

Imagine a person becoming a leader for the first time. It is unlikely that the person will have all the skills needed immediately. There is a need for more sophisticated leadership training courses that will help new leaders see where their weaknesses lie; in this way they can get appropriate training or even receive cooperative assistance within their own organization so that they will not falter as they start their new roles.

A lot has been done recently on peer-pairing relationships for new executives. A new executive will immediately be paired off with a peer with more experience so that the experienced person can help the newcomer move into the role with a minimum of difficulty by helping to supplement his or her skills. By creating such a pair relationship using peer or retired leaders the four skills can be supplemented until such time as the new leader has sufficient experience.

## Questions To Be Addressed

The over-all model of course raises many questions. One major issue that is often raised is: In this schema hierarchical? Is it not like Maslow's hierarchy of needs, suggesting that the fourth phase is better than the others?

This is a difficult question that cannot be addressed fully here. I would like to speak to it briefly, however, in order to get the four skills of the confluent theory in perspective. The model is not basically hierarchical as much as it is developmental. People grow at a natural rate and learn through the processes of selecting the alternatives available to them.

The fact is that institutions (family, school, business) reinforce individual development. And in turn a civilization as a whole reinforces the institutions of any particular society. That is to say a particular point in history will in fact be reinforcing persons at a particular developmental level. Excluding the very exceptional and unusual persons, such as Buddha or Christ or Socrates who somehow symbolize humanity's future potential, the majority of people like ourselves can only grow to that phase of development that is openly reinforced by our society. To reinforce a phase means of course to reinforce through education all the skills necessary to make it behaviorally possible.

The point is that values that precipitate out of the phase of development in which we find ourselves are not so much hierarchical but are the limits imposed by the conditions of history itself. Simply put, the fourth phase of development as spelled out in this essay is as far as we can see at this point, as far as our present history and imaginal skills allow us to see. In this respect I am talking about the present authors and their limited vision; maybe other persons who read this can see further than that phase.

### An Example in Guatemala

I am reminded of working in a rural area in Guatemala a number of years ago where the malnutrition rate was more than fifty percent, the unemployment was high and the ability of the local population to make a reasonable living was depressingly low. Disease was often rampant and life expectancy was in the early thirties.

A leader was required for a local Episcopal mission. One of our tasks was to go to that area and give some counseling to the person who was running the mission, which included a local clinic, a school and an agricultural plantation. Being somewhat naive at that time, I considered the individual who was in charge of the mission to be an insensitive person who lacked many of the skills that one would obviously expect of a middle-class Anglo-Saxon.

However as I reviewed the situation over a period of years I became convinced that the so-called "sensitive Anglo-Saxon" would never survive in such a situation. His level of development would be inhibiting to the people—would be wholly unhelpful in fact and would probably cause him and his family to get physically ill.

The developmental state of that particular area required leadership that would understand the situation and be able to deal with it. To speak as I often did with this man about values like honesty, trust, construction, relaxation and leisure for a new world was simply ludicrous. There was no communication. He was living in a world of violence and of history; the natural environment itself was reinforcing a survival existence. The humanizing process required a person who could reinforce people where they were and assist them in moving to a new stage of development. A new level of development has to be merely one stage ahead of where the people presently find themselves. It is not a question of hierarchy, it is a question of value development within the limits and context of history. People are where they are concretely in a particular society.

## The Integrated Person

Another question that is raised continually is: Are we not all at different stages on the values scale at various times? And are not our skills at different phases? An integrated person is one whose behavior reflects his or her values at one phase and who has all the skills needed to express those values with the imagination being at least a stage ahead of that point. However this does not speak to the question of whether or not we can move down the scale as well as up it. And can this upward and downward movement happen on a day-to-day or week-to-week basis?

Generally speaking I think we usually stay where we are and move forward very slowly in the developmental process. But environment can change and a person can temporarily drop into a much lower phase of development. This of course has confusing consequences because the imagination is not totally reduced even though the behavior might suddenly be, in which case momentary confusing behavior is manifested.

In short, situations can move us up and down the value scale. The loss of a job, the sudden declaration of war between one society and another, or, even on the positive side, suddenly being given an award or receiving a degree or getting a new job can move a person forward on the scale with new responsibilities and a new vision for the world. These things do move us up and down the scale but I would claim that there is a steady core of development to which we can generally relate. And we do this in an educational setting by concentrating on the development of the values expressive of where we are and on the development of the appropriate skills so that we can develop in a holistic manner.

## Conclusion

We need to be able to look at the world in a more integrated and holistic fashion. Far too often methods of teaching, styles of leadership and even ways of healing people have been too narrowly confined to one set of skills to the neglect of the others or to one set of values to the neglect of the others.

For example often people in counseling have stressed the need for interpersonal skills and for values like honesty and trust. These things are essential to the development of an individual's mental health, but they are only a part of a whole. Other values and skills are needed. A counselor from a psychological background in order to be in touch with some other values like harmony or construction may need to learn about engineering and the arts as well as about psychology.

Similarly, in education one teacher may be very enthusiastic about behavior modification as a means of aiding students. Another may be devoted to cognitive development, trying to convey a great deal of information to the child. In the latter case the instrumental skills receive nearly exclusive attention, a tendency that has constituted the main thrust of traditional education. There has been little effort, for example, to acquaint teachers with the kinds of skills they might gainfully use in dealing with the educational system itself. Teachers need to confront themselves with questions like: "Do I use this educational method because I'm convinced it is the best or does it merely reflect where I am developmentally? What new skills do I need?"

An awareness of the four skills and of their relationship to values can help us to see things more holistically. We have all the skills we need in the present world. All the values that we speak of are operative. They simply need to be brought into harmony and integrated into the individual person and into the institutions of society.

1. Ivan Illich, *Tools for Conviviality.* New York: Harper & Row, 1973.
2. Paolo Soleri, *The Arcology of Paolo Soleri.* Cambridge, Mass.: The MIT Press, 1972.
3. Lawrence Kohlberg, in C. M. Beck, B. S. Crittenden and E. V. Sullivan (eds.), *Moral Education.* Toronto: University of Toronto Press, 1971.
4. Erik Erikson, *Childhood and Society.* New York: Norton, 1963.
5. Gordon W. Allport, *The Nature of Prejudice.* Menlo Park, Calif.: Addison-Wesley Co., 1954.
6. Thomas C. Oden, *Game Free: A Guide to the Meaning of Intimacy.* New York: Harper & Row, 1974.
7. Salvador Minuchin, *et al., Families of the Slums: An Exploration of Their Structure Treatment.* New York: Basic Books, 1967.
8. Virginia Satir, *Conjoint Family Therapy.* Palo Alto, California: Science and Behavior Books, Inc., 1967.

# PART II:
# CHARTING ONE'S CONSCIOUSNESS TRACK

In the process of personal growth, one must deal with three basic questions:

1. Where am I now?
2. Where would I like to be?
3. How can I move toward my goal?

This section is intended to help the individual develop a practical plan for personal growth by using Hall's methods for clarifying one's values, charting one's consciousness track and assessing one's skills.

We hold our values at different levels of awareness. Some values are fully assimilated, internalized, taken for granted—what we call "act" values. They are part of our meaning system, are manifested in our customary behavior, are evident even when we must act under pressure. At the same time, we aspire toward other values, toward an envisioned ideal self not yet really embodied in our daily lives. This ideal self represents what we call our "vision" values.

In between the act values and the vision values is the area of conscious choice, the area of struggle with the priorities that preoccupy us in the present moment. We are able to put them into action when we are not under pressure, but need both more skills and more practice to internalize them. As we develop the skills necessary to achieve our "choice" values, these priorities become internalized and we move closer to our aspirations.

To express this sequence in another way, in attempting to acquire a new value or a new behavior, we move through the following stages:

1. *The unconscious incompetent.* We don't know and we are unaware of our ignorance. Thus, the person with a Phase I consciousness does not perceive a Phase III value.
2. *The conscious incompetent.* We are aware of our ignorance or lack—the new value presents itself.

3. *The conscious competent.* If we give our full attention to the task, we are able to achieve the new behavior or actualize the new value. We are in the area of choice. But in a stress situation, we will most probably revert to our old behavior.
4. *The unconscious competent.* The new value is fully internalized; we behave accordingly, even under pressure—it has become second nature, an act value.

In this section we proceed through the following steps:

a. Exploring our values through a series of initial exercises.
b. Using the Time Diary to analyze our daily activities and generate a series of value priorities.
c. Constructing a personal consciousness track on the basis of these value priorities and using it to identify act, choice and vision values.
d. Assessing our levels of skill development in the four skill areas.
e. Developing a personal growth contract in the light of the data and insights about the self arising from steps a through d.

## A. Exploratory Exercises*

### 1. IDENTIFYING ACT AND CHOICE VALUES

*Objective:*

**To identify act and choice values in three specific areas.**

a. The seven marks on the continuum below indicate a seven point scale, from (1) for unimportant to (7) for earth-shattering.

*Contributed by Mark Young

| Money | | / | / | / | / | / | / | / |
|---|---|---|---|---|---|---|---|---|
| | | 1 | 2 | 3 | 4 | 5 | 6 | 7 |

| Education | | / | / | / | / | / | / | / |
|---|---|---|---|---|---|---|---|---|
| | | 1 | 2 | 3 | 4 | 5 | 6 | 7 |

| Religion | | / | / | / | / | / | / | / |
|---|---|---|---|---|---|---|---|---|
| | | 1 | 2 | 3 | 4 | 5 | 6 | 7 |

| Other | | / | / | / | / | / | / | / |
|---|---|---|---|---|---|---|---|---|
| | | 1 | 2 | 3 | 4 | 5 | 6 | 7 |

Spend a few minutes brainstorming three or four key words which describe what these concepts mean to you. Write them down in the space below:

Money:

Education:

Religion:

Other:

b. Now place the letter "c" (choice value) on each scale at the point that indicates how important you believe money, or education, or religion *ought* to be in your life, according to your standards.

   Then place the letter "a" (act value) on each continuum at the point that indicates how you actually behave in your daily life with respect to that area. For instance, I may put my "c" or choice value with regard to religion at $6\frac{1}{2}$, yet I spend little time or energy going to church or engaging in religious activities, so I place my "a" at $1\frac{1}{2}$.

c. Subtract the act values from the choice values. In the above example, $6\frac{1}{2} - 1\frac{1}{2} = 5$. If the difference is large, you may have difficulty in making choices in that area. If you have a number of divergent scores in various areas of your life, you will probably experience discouragement, frustration, and feelings of disappointment in yourself.

d. Share your scores with a partner or small group.

e. Discuss:

   • Compare your definitions of the areas in step "a" with each other. Do they coincide or diverge? What do you think this means?

   • Compare your scores on each value with the others in the group. Whose "c" scores are most different from yours? Are these the people with whom you experience the most conflict?

   • Describe a conflict you have had recently with someone. Was it a conflict of values?

*Variation:* Think of areas of your life where you are feeling confused or are experiencing difficulty in making choices. Construct value continuums for these areas. Does this help you to clarify your options?

## 2. PERSONAL VALUES AND FAMILY VALUES

It is often said that values are "caught not taught," and, of course, our family members are the first persons to impress their values upon us. The following exercise can be used to examine the influence of family members on our values.

*Objective:*

**To explore the influence of family members on my value choices.**

a. On a separate sheet, for each member of the family you grew up with, draw three continuums for the three areas in Exercise 1—money, education, religion. Place the letters "c" and "a" where you believe the choices and actions would fall for that particular person.

b. Reflect on the following:

- Whose values are closest to yours?
- Is that the person whom you have felt closest to in your family?
- Whose values are most dissimilar to yours?
- Is this the person with whom you have the most conflict?

- Whose values most strongly influenced you?
- Is there anyone in your family you might have strongly influenced?
- Is there anyone in your family you would like to share this exercise with?

## 3. IDEALS AND VALUES

An interesting way to explore the concept of vision in the development of values is to investigate our best-loved characters in fiction. This exercise is designed to discern the basic traits of some of these characters. They are apt to embody our vision of the person we would like to become as well as the skills to which we aspire.

*Objective:*

**To get in touch with our ideal self.**

a. Write down three of your favorite characters in fiction. They may be taken from novels, films, plays, or fairy tales. On the chart below, list three or four characteristics of each of your choices.

b. Now turn to the values list on pp. 67-68 and find the closest counterparts for each of these characteristics, and jot them down on the chart.

## Characters for Ex. 3

1. _____

Characteristics

_____

_____

_____

Values

_____

_____

_____

2. _____

Characteristics

_____

_____

_____

Values

_____

_____

_____

3. _____

Characteristics

_____

_____

_____

Values

_____

_____

_____

c. Share with a partner or a small group. Describe the qualities of your characters, and see if your partner(s) can guess which characters you chose if you give them the title of the work as a clue.

d. Discuss:

- To what extent do these qualities of your characters represent your ideal self?
- What skills do these characters possess that you would like to acquire? (Note that if the characters represent envisioned values, it is likely that you will possess relatively few of the skills in their repertoires.)
- Do all three of your characters represent some particular kind of achievement? Do they share any value? If so, how relevant is this value to you?

e. Repeat this exercise, this time using real people from history, present-day public life, or your personal circle.

# B. Time Diary*

Consider time as the focus of values and meaning. What we do takes time. Time, however, is also a way of describing what we do and to whom we relate. It is these two elements that constitute all meaning in life. For each twenty-four hours, you will have exchanged one day of your life. Only you can determine each day's worth.

## 1. DIRECTIONS FOR KEEPING A TIME DIARY

The purpose of the Time Diary is to enable people to become aware of how they use time, and how they might choose to utilize time more advantageously. We recommend keeping a daily diary for one month. It is important to follow the instructions carefully so that maximum value can be gained from this instrument. Use the Daily Time Report Form (cf. p. 43) to record your daily activities together with the names of individuals or groups with whom the time was spent. Count only your waking hours spent in actual communication with an individual as time spent with that person. Sleep does not count as time spent with a person. The example below illustrates the procedure.

## Categories of Time*

Identify how your time each day can be placed in the following categories: work, play, maintenance and freesence. Add up the amount of time spent in each type of activity and round off to the nearest half hour as in the example below.

| | |
|---|---|
| Work | 4½ hrs. |
| Play | 5 |
| Maintenance | 7 |
| Freesence | ½ |
| Sleep | 7 |
| | = 24 hours |

*Work:* What you do that effects change in your environment. Work occurs during a limited number of hours, at a specific place, for a specific purpose. During work you are producing and coping. You will be interacting with fellow students, co-workers, institutional representatives, and, in some cases, customers or clients. You are concerned with duty, obligation, and the expectations of others.

Work may include your profession, a paid or salaried occupation, or activities as a student. It may also include special vocational arrangements, such as a part-time job, housework or continuous volunteer work.

*Maintenance:* What you do to:

a. Recuperate from work.
b. Maintain the physical and emotional well-being of yourself and others.
c. Maintain your home and possessions.

Maintenance occurs during an identifiable amount of time. It involves resting, recuperating, and upkeep. During maintenance there is heavy emphasis on your bodily needs, and because maintenance time will include time spent recuperating from work, it will include such activities as playing a game of tennis or having a beer and relaxing at the end of a hard day. Maintenance will also include:

---

*Developed by Larry Rosen and Patricia Alexander, based on the "IF Diary" of Brian Hall.

*For further discussion of these categories see Brian P. Hall, *Value Clarification as Learning Process.* N.Y.: Paulist Press, 1973, pp. 22–29, 215–216, 245–281.

## Daily Time Report

| TIME | ACTIVITY | W/PERSON | TIME | ACTIVITY | W/PERSON |
|---|---|---|---|---|---|
| 7 AM | woke up | self | 7 PM | saw | Pam |
| 8 | bath breakfast | | 8 | movie on | |
| 9 | drove to class | self | 9 | T.V. | |
| 10 | study | self | 10 | | |
| 11 | History class | Fellow students | 11 | Cleaned Room | self |
| 12 | Studied in Library | Self | 12 | | |
| | Lunch | Janet & Bruce | | | |
| 1 PM | Psychology Class | Fellow Students | 1 AM | Sleep | self |
| 2 | | | 2 | | |
| 3 | Played ping pong | Pat | | | |
| 4 | | | 4 | | |
| 5 | Drove home | self | 5 | | |
| 6 | Cooked | self | 6 | | |
| | Dinner | Pam | | | |

a. Travel time (commuting) to and from work.
b. Extending work, such as studying with friends, driving people somewhere.
c. Maintenance of special property, such as checking out or returning library books, getting car fixed.
d. Time spent on health and hygiene, from diet or exercise to bathing.
e. Time spent on duties and obligations to care for and maintain family, friends.
f. Caring for property outside your profession or trade.
g. Emotional maintenance of persons *at* school. Listening to others' problems. Helping another person to cope.
h. Emotional maintenance of persons *outside* of school or work; this would include family, friends.

*Play:* Play is the opposite of work in that it does not involve duty or obligation. Usually, play is having fun by acting in a way different from the way you act during work. Play occurs at planned times and places. It involves fantasizing, searching and celebrating. Play involves choosing those with whom we wish to spend time, not out of duty or expectations of others. We may often be intimate with our playmates. During play we often explore and act out our fantasies and hopes. It is a time for fun and socializing, and demands sharing and trustful relationships. Play may include occasional excess.

*Freesence:* Freesence occurs at a high level of consciousness. It involves a being with, and contemplation of the environment. During freesence, time becomes unlimited; a moment may seem like an hour or an hour like a moment. One becomes totally a part of one's environment and experiences at-one-ness with surroundings. Freesence involves being, waiting and seeing. Whether alone or with another person, one experiences intimacy and unity.

Freesence involves activities that move toward intimacy or solitude. Time is unprogrammed, but regularly allotted for. Examples might include sexual play, reading poetry, looking at a work of art, a walk alone in the woods—during which you feel at one with nature, or a deeply meaningful, spiritual or religious experience. Freesence is celebration, festivity and meaning.

*Sleep:* Means that *you are asleep.* This includes time dreaming, not daydreaming, and napping. It may be that you sleep with someone, but during actual sleep you are alone. You may wish to record your dreams in the "feelings" section of your diary. Sleep is usually considered a form of maintenance, but for the purpose of this diary, we are considering it separately.

# DAILY PERCEPTIONS

Indicate each day your perception of how the day went, relative to whether it was one of your best days or one of your worst days, whether you learned a great deal or learned nothing, and whether or not you did what you wanted to.

## Daily Feelings

Record those experiences you had during the day which were significant. These experiences may be either positive or negative. Identify the feelings these experiences generated within you. Discuss problems you are dealing with, and brainstorm possible solutions. To write at least seventy words will help you to reflect upon your day.

*Today Was:*

| | | | | | | |
|---|---|---|---|---|---|---|
| The Best Day of My Life | ( ) | (X) | ( ) | ( ) | ( ) | The Worst Day of My Life |
| I Learned a Great Deal | ( ) | (X) | ( ) | ( ) | ( ) | I Learned Nothing |
| I Did What I Wanted To Do | ( ) | ( ) | ( ) | (X) | ( ) | I Did Not Do What I Wanted To Do |

*(Example)*
How Do You *Feel* Today? (In 70 words or more)

*Tired, but it's a good feeling because I was able to be outdoors, in the sunshine after so many dreary winter days in a row.*

*Wish I could decide which classes to take this quarter. There are a lot of things to consider, but I think I'll feel better once the decision is made.*

*Family problems are taking their toll on my peace of mind, but I am unable to change the situation and am working on accepting things the way they are, for now.*

*Please Note:* Be open and honest with yourself. If you plan to share this diary with others, simply mark out with a black magic marker those sections that are too personal to share. This will enable you to be completely open with yourself, and yet preserve your privacy.

Date: _____    WORK    _____
Day of Week: _____    PLAY    _____
                                             MAINTENANCE   _____
                                             FREESENCE     _____
                                             SLEEP         _____
                                                             = 24 hours

## Daily Time Report

| Time | Activity | W/Person |
|------|----------|----------|
| 7 AM | | |
| 8 | | |
| 9 | | |
| 10 | | |
| 11 | | |
| 12 | | |
| 1 PM | | |
| 2 | | |
| 3 | | |
| 4 | | |
| 5 | | |
| 6 | | |
| 7 PM | | |
| 8 | | |
| 9 | | |
| 10 | | |
| 11 | | |
| 12 | | |
| 1 AM | | |
| 2 | | |
| 3 | | |
| 4 | | |
| 5 | | |
| 6 | | |

**Today Was:**

| The Best Day of My Life | ( ) | ( ) | ( ) | ( ) | ( ) | The Worst Day of My Life |
| I Learned a Great Deal | ( ) | ( ) | ( ) | ( ) | ( ) | I Learned Nothing |
| I Did What I Wanted To Do | ( ) | ( ) | ( ) | ( ) | ( ) | I Did Not Do What I Wanted To Do |

How Do You *Feel* Today? (In 70 words or more)

## 2. Analysis: Time

### Calculations

Calculate the number of hours spent during the month (in which you kept the diary) in each of the following categories: work, play, maintenance, freesence and sleep. Figure the percentage of time spent in each category by dividing the number of hours in each by the total number of hours for the month. (Since in actuality, you have kept your diary for four weeks, or 28 days, the total number of hours in the month will equal 24 hours $\times$ 28 days or 672 hours.)

Total Hours at Work        % of Total Time

[  ] $\div$ 672 = [  ]

Total Hours at Maintenance

[  ] $\div$ 672 = [  ]

Total Hours at Play

[  ] $\div$ 672 = [  ]

Total Hours at Freesence

[  ] $\div$ 672 = [  ]

Total Hours Asleep

[  ] $\div$ 672 = [  ]

### Questions

Answer the following questions:

1. Am I satisfied with my over-all use of time or do I wish to make some changes? _____

2. Am I experiencing conflict between my home and school life? _____
If yes, explain.

3. Do my work hours exceed 60 hours per week? (Or 36% of my total time.) _____
If yes, identify cause.

4. Do I have a minimal amount of freesence? (Freesence of at least 3 hours per week or 2% of total time.)
_____
If no, explain why.

5. Do I have a minimal amount of maintenance? (At least 30 hours or 18% of total time.) _____
If no, explain why.

6. How do I know that my life is not simply a meaningless activity?

## Interpretation of Your Responses to the Time Analysis Questions

The places where you spend most of your time indicate where your priority relationships are, and where your priority values are. Little time spent in play or in freesence indicates limited ability to be intimate with others. Creativity, contemplation, and intimacy can only emerge out of play and freesence. A heavy maintenance schedule, for example, would perhaps indicate values of care and service rather than intimacy and creativity.

The purpose of this interpretation is not to judge, but to discern what is the most appropriate and harmonious way for you. This interpretation refers only to the way you use your time; however, it represents an indication of what to expect of yourself, what is most meaningful to you, and some of the ways you can achieve more harmonious relationships.

1. "Am I satisfied with my overall use of time or do I wish to make some changes? If so, how do I begin?"

   a. Make changes slowly and carefully, for to make a change in one area will alter the whole system.
   b. If a change in work time is desired, be realistic as to whether this is possible at the present time. Make sure that this is not really a question of maintenance. Careful planning is essential.
   c. An excessive amount of maintenance of self and possessions may reflect inadequate skill in relating to other persons, and may indicate the need for a change in maintenance time. Excessive emotional maintenance of others may indicate neglect of one's own needs or low self-esteem, or need to have others dependent on one, and can be very draining and needs to be countered by the opposite type of experience, such as vigorous physical exercise.
   d. Freesence is a quality that emerges only beyond play. If we note a lack of freesence time, some things that may require attention are; close and intimate friendships—outside of work/school related activities, skilled or disciplined activities such as advanced hobbies, and meditation.

2. "Am I experiencing conflict between my home and school/work life?" Are my hours of work and maintenance at school/work, traveling, or away from home, taking something away from my family life? For the single person: Am I spending enough time with close friends?

   a. Long hours at work may indicate avoidance of close relationships with family or friends. Intimacy is essential to personal development, and if it is lacking, I need to think about the quality of relationships.
   b. If maintenance at school or work is high, tension may result, since family members need attention also. If we are emotionally drained when we come home, our family may feel antagonistic toward our work/school as a consequence.
   c. When both persons in a relationship have high maintenance in their work/school, tension is bound to result unless careful planning is given to areas of play or freesence of an intimate nature.

3. "Do my work hours tend to exceed 60 hours per week?" If so attention should be given to this fact, and rigorous attention given to play, meditation, and physical exercise. This is particularly true if maintenance is primarily emotional. Students should be concerned about excessive eating, sleeping or social drinking.

4. "Do I have a minimal amount of freesence?" Low freesence is not a problem unless play is also low or absent. The absence of both would indicate possible health problems. Low freesence raises a question as to the quality of our relationships. Since freesence is a consequence of consciousness (maturity) and skill, its absence might suggest that ways of growth and development in terms of time and skill need to be explored. Without quality time to oneself in freesence, it is difficult to reflect on what is happening, to be in touch with one's feelings, and to set appropriate goals for oneself.

5. "Do I have a minimal amount of maintenance?" Absence of maintenance would suggest that the inventory was not properly understood. Low maintenance is not serious unless you have health problems.

6. "How do I know that my life is effective and not simply a meaningless activity?"

   a. If my life exhibits a balance between intimacy in human relationships, solitude and meaning in time alone, and satisfaction in significant work.
   b. If I have enough play and freesence time, for these provide the opportunity for meaning making or the ability to make sense of my life.
   c. If I exhibit creative talent. (However, if I do not show well-developed personal relationships in the play area, I may need to address the possibility that I am avoiding human relationships.)
   d. Freesence represents a high level of development; care should be taken not to confuse it with play. Persons with low amounts or absence of freesence can find meaning making possible with disciplined times of solitude and at least minimal intimacy with their peers.

Freesence time becomes a quality space if:

- you have a high capacity to function in the here and now, so that your unique potential can emerge;
- you can creatively resolve conflicts and solve problems;
- if you maintain proper perspective and understand the relative importance of the different areas of work, play, maintenance, and freesence.

## Time and Your Values

From the List of Values on pp. 67-68   identify those values you see reflected in your use of time.

Most Important Values

(Identify from the list of values the five values which were most important in your decisions about how to use your time.)

Other Important Values

(Identify from the list of values any other values you consider important in your decision about how to use your time.)

## 3. ANALYSIS: PERSONS

*Persons:* Calculate number of hours spent with each person or group of persons. Rank, in order of hours spent with each, the persons with whom you spent the most time.

| Person 1 | | Total Hours | | % of Total Time |
|---|---|---|---|---|
| [ ] | ÷ | 672 | = | [ ] |
| Person 2 | | | | |
| [ ] | ÷ | 672 | = | [ ] |
| Person 3 | | | | |
| [ ] | ÷ | 672 | = | [ ] |
| Person 4 | | | | |
| [ ] | ÷ | 672 | = | [ ] |
| Person 5 | | | | |
| [ ] | ÷ | 672 | = | [ ] |

### Questions:
Answer the following questions:

1. Do the results of this section surprise you?

2. Are you satisfied with the amount of time you spent with others? Explain your reply.

3. If not satisfied, what changes would you make?

4. Brainstorm two strategies to bring about any desired change.

### Persons and Your Values
From the List of Values on pp. 67-68 identify those values reflected in your choices of persons with whom you spend time.

| Most Important Values | Other Important Values |
|---|---|
| _____ | _____ |
| _____ | _____ |
| _____ | _____ |
| _____ | _____ |

## 4. ANALYSIS: DAILY PERCEPTIONS

Re-examine your daily perceptions and respond to the following questions:

How do you feel about the month? Place a ✓ in the appropriate places.

1. The Best Month of My Life                                          Worst Month of My Life

_____

2. A Month in Which I Learned                                        A Month in Which I
a Great Deal                                                          Learned Nothing

_____

3. A Month in Which I                                                A Month in Which I Did
Did What I Wanted                                                    Not Do What I Wanted

_____

4. Are you satisfied with the results of the preceding questions?

5. How might you change your use of time to improve the results?

## 5. ANALYSIS: FEELINGS
Re-read your recordings of daily feelings and respond to the following questions:

1. What feelings occurred most frequently during this month? Why?

2. What was the most significant problem with which you had to deal?

3. During which day of the month were you most happy, and which day were you most unhappy? Why?

4. Did you find this diary helpful in clarifying and dealing with your problems and accomplishing your personal objectives?

### Feelings and Your Values
From the List of Values on pp. 67-68 identify those values that seem to underlie your feelings and those values that are apparent in any conflicts or problems.

| Most Important Values | Other Important Values |
| --- | --- |
| | |
| | |
| | |
| | |
| | |
| | |

## C. Construction of Your Consciousness Track

### Step 1. Identifying Phases and Stages, Primary and Means Values

On page 69 you will find an instrument called *Phases and Stages of Consciousness,* which places our list of eighty-eight values on a chart according to the four phases and eight stages of value development. Each phase has an "A" and a "B" stage. The values in the "A" stage center around personal attitudes and activities and can be expressed within a private sphere. The values in the "B" stage focus outward toward institutions and therefore tend to be expressed in the public sphere. Thus, personal growth as an individual value is placed in stage III A, whereas mutual accountability, having a public character, falls under III B. Generally, a person moving into a new phase of consciousness will tend to acquire the more personal values before the institutional values.

Each column on the chart is divided into a top and bottom section. In the top section are the long-term priorities or primary values, the values that make up a person's core of meaning at a given stage. In the bottom section are the short-term priorities or means values. Thus, self-worth is a long-term priority, a value that always remains important to us in a conscious way. Orderliness is a short-term priority, involving a definite set of skills. Once we have acquired the skills

of keeping things in order, they become habitual and we need not devote conscious effort to them. The long-term priorities are our goals. The short-term priorities are our objectives.

To construct your personal consciousness track, go through the following steps:

1. List the values you have identified as being important in your diary. Any values which have occurred more than once should be considered important.

| Most Important Values | Code |
|---|---|
| _____ | • ___ |
| _____ | • ___ |
| _____ | • ___ |
| _____ | • ___ |
| _____ | • ___ |
| _____ | • ___ |
| _____ | • ___ |
| _____ | • ___ |
| _____ | • ___ |
| _____ | • ___ |

## Personal Consciousness Track

| | I A | I B | II A | II B | III A | III B | IV A | IV B |
|---|---|---|---|---|---|---|---|---|
| Primary Values or Goals | | | | | | | | |
| Means Values or Objectives | | | | | | | | |

| Other Important Values | Code |
|---|---|
| _____ | • _____ |
| _____ | • _____ |
| _____ | • _____ |
| _____ | • _____ |
| _____ | • _____ |
| _____ | • _____ |
| _____ | • _____ |
| _____ | • _____ |
| _____ | • _____ |
| _____ | • _____ |

2. Code each value according to its phase and stage. For example, empathy is III A.

3. Code each value as either primary (Pr)—on top of the column, or means (Me)—on the bottom of the column,

4. Now place all your values on your own consciousness track, each in its right place—that is, phase, stage, top or bottom.

## Step 2. Identifying Act, Choice and Vision Values

Some of your values will be more indicative of where you would like to be than where you actually are. These are your *aspirations or visions*. Other priorities are ones that perhaps you are aware of but for the most part they are taking care of themselves. For example: "Belonging" might be important to you but for the most part you feel this is taken care of. This is what we call *act*—it is being done already. Finally, there is a large area in the middle called *choice* values. These are the value priorities that occupy our minds most of the time but could use improvement. Empathy, for example, is a value we may try to implement, but perhaps feel we could use more skills in this area. The accompanying diagram will illustrate this further.

Choice values are the ones I can follow when I am not under pressure. But when I am in a new situation or under pressure, I find that the values are not internalized sufficiently for me to *act* them out without a great deal of conscious effort. *Act values* are those that are a part of my behavior no matter what the pressure. As I develop the skills of my *choice values* and these priorities become internalized as *act values,* so I grow toward my *vision* or *aspired values.*

To complete the charting of your consciousness track, it is necessary to decide which value priorities are *act,* which are *choice,* and which are *vision.* This is partly arbitrary. First, look at the highest value cluster and bracket it—these are your vision values. Next, take the lowest cluster and bracket it—these are your act values. The center cluster will be your choice area and will normally span only two stages.

## *Values as Act — Choice — Vision*

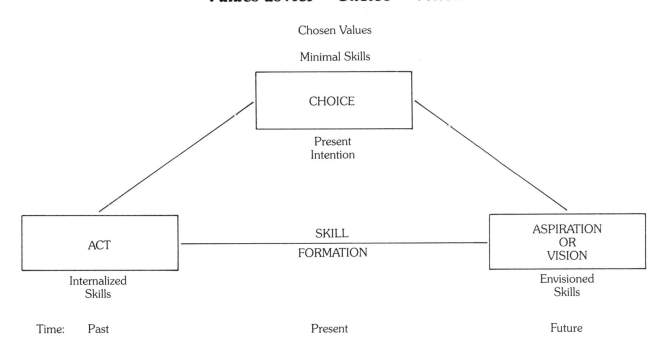

*(Example)*

| | I | | | II | | | III | | | IV | |
|---|---|---|---|---|---|---|---|---|---|---|---|
| A | | B | A | | B | A | | B | A | | B |
| | | security | belonging | | competence | service vocation | | | | | |
| | | | courtesy | | control of others<br><br>achieve-ment | empathy<br><br><br>trust | | | mutual accounta-bility coopera-tion | | inter-dependence |

Act        Choice        Vision

In the above example, you can see that the main cluster is in II B/III A and is central; therefore, it becomes choice.

Take your consciousness track and bracket *act, choice* and *vision.*

## Step 3. Questions To Consider

1. Are your vision values ones which you do not know how to achieve?

2. What values are you having the most difficulty with? List them below:

_____

_____

_____

_____

_____

Are these the values in your choice area?

3. When your choice cluster is more than one stage apart from the choice cluster of someone you work with, the communication may be seriously hindered. Do you experience such problems or conflicts with other persons? Describe them.

4. If your main choice values are in Phase II, conflict may arise easily with persons who have Phase I or Phase III values. Do you recognize such difficulties in your life? Illustrate.

5. When your choice cluster is between II B and III A as in the example, conflict often occurs between personal creativity and independence and what the system (e.g., the university) requires. Are you aware of such conflict? Describe.

6. Persons whose values are III B/IV A and who are highly rational may be misreading their value level, especially if their interpersonal skills are low. Do you know of such instances? Should you recheck your value level?

## D. Skills Inventory*

We can look at behavior in two ways: (1) as an indication of values—e.g., the way I spend my time is a reliable indication of the values actually operative in my daily life; (2) as the product of a skill which a person is acquiring or has acquired. Values are internalized as one becomes skilled in the related behaviors. I take pride in my craftsmanship as I master my tools; and conversely, as my skills increase, I perceive new possibilities of meaning and value. As my skill with the violin improves, my ear becomes more sensitive and my appreciation of a Itzak Perlman grows.

In working toward a realistic personal growth contract, it is useful to look at behavior in both of the above ways. Up to this point, we have been analyzing behavior in order to clarify our values. In charting the consciousness track, we have identified our act, choice and vision values, and thus can answer the first two questions with which Part II began, namely: (1) Where am I now? and (2) Where would I like to be?

*Developed by Janet Kalven and Kenneth Prunty on the basis of Brian Hall's analysis of the four skill areas.

We are now in a position to tackle question (3) How can I move toward my goals? The crucial next step is to connect my choice values with the requisite skills. No doubt we have all experienced the futility of moral exhortations from others or blame from oneself so far as changing behavior is concerned. But if I can identify the skills needed to achieve the new behaviors that accord with my desired values, then I can focus my energies on specific, attainable targets.

The *Values List* already relates the values to the four broad skill areas. However, a more detailed assessment of one's present skills is useful in pinpointing specific weaknesses where further skill development will help to internalize new values. Hence, the following inventory.

On the four lists which follow, you are asked to evaluate yourself with regard to each specific skill according to the scale below. For each skill, circle the appropriate score.

0 = I have no skill in this area
1 = I have minimal skill in this area
2 = I have average skill in this area
3 = I have strong, well-developed skill

# 1. INSTRUMENTAL SKILLS

*Instrumental Skills:* the abilities that enable one to get a job done; the intellectual and physical competencies that enable one to shape both ideas and the immediate external environment; the skills involved in physical dexterity, handicrafts, and cognitive accomplishments.

| Skill | Score |
|---|---|
| 1. Coordinating one's physical self in some form of sport or exercise. | 0 1 2 3 |
| 2. Speaking effectively about what one thinks and feels in a one-to-one setting. | 0 1 2 3 |
| 3. Speaking effectively about what one thinks and feels in a small group setting. | 0 1 2 3 |
| 4. Speaking effectively about what one thinks and feels before a large audience. | 0 1 2 3 |
| 5. Listening attentively and paraphrasing accurately. | 0 1 2 3 |
| 6. Expressing one's thoughts and feelings clearly and forcefully in writing personal letters or diaries. | 0 1 2 3 |
| 7. Expressing one's thoughts and feelings clearly and effectively in writing memos and reports. | 0 1 2 3 |
| 8. Expressing one's thoughts, feelings, and observations in poetic or fictional form. | 0 1 2 3 |
| 9. Using a large and discriminating vocabulary. | 0 1 2 3 |
| 10. Reading quickly and with comprehension newspapers, periodicals, light fiction. | 0 1 2 3 |
| 11. Reading poetry and serious fiction with comprehension. | 0 1 2 3 |
| 12. Reading research reports and scholarly works with comprehension. | 0 1 2 3 |
| 13. Participating effectively in role playing. | 0 1 2 3 |
| 14. Identifying and constructing role plays suitable for a given group. | 0 1 2 3 |
| 15. Able to use mathematical techniques to synthesize and present data. | 0 1 2 3 |
| 16. Able to make and manage budgets. | 0 1 2 3 |
| 17. Able to manage one's time and prioritize activities. | 0 1 2 3 |
| 18. Able to research a topic or question and summarize findings clearly and cogently. | 0 1 2 3 |
| 19. Able to analyze and criticize another's argument. | 0 1 2 3 |
| 20. Able to marshal evidence and frame arguments in support of a position. | 0 1 2 3 |
| 21. Able to master new skills in one's job. | 0 1 2 3 |
| 22. Able to plan for and carry out learning activities for oneself. | 0 1 2 3 |
| 23. Able to plan and carry out learning activities for others. | 0 1 2 3 |
| 24. Able to utilize active and involving modes of learning: games, simulations, role plays, experience-based exercises, etc. | 0 1 2 3 |
| 25. Able to plan for and facilitate meetings. | 0 1 2 3 |
| 26. Able to utilize a variety of problem-solving techniques. | 0 1 2 3 |
| 27. Able to identify problem areas and define problems. | 0 1 2 3 |
| 28. Able to use ordinary household tools, e.g., hammer, screwdriver, plunger, kitchen utensils, paint brush. | 0 1 2 3 |
| 29. Able to use modern machines and technologies, e.g., drive a car, use a calculator, use office machines, etc. | 0 1 2 3 |
| 30. Able to observe and record accurately small and large group interactions. | 0 1 2 3 |

Take the total numerical value of the numbers you have circled and write it here.

## 2. INTERPERSONAL SKILLS

*Interpersonal Skills:* the ability to perceive self and others accurately, in ways that facilitate communication, mutual understanding and cooperation.

| **Skill** | | **Score** | | |
|---|---|---|---|---|
| 1. Identifying my own feelings accurately. | 0 | 1 | 2 | 3 |
| 2. Identifying another's feelings accurately. | 0 | 1 | 2 | 3 |
| 3. Expressing my feelings openly. | 0 | 1 | 2 | 3 |
| 4. Accepting my own worth, feeling happy with myself. | 0 | 1 | 2 | 3 |
| 5. Being aware of my "self-talk," i.e., my expectations of myself. | 0 | 1 | 2 | 3 |
| 6. Accepting my limitations peacefully. | 0 | 1 | 2 | 3 |
| 7. Identifying and expressing my negative feelings. | 0 | 1 | 2 | 3 |
| 8. Accepting positive feedback non-apologetically. | 0 | 1 | 2 | 3 |
| 9. Accepting negative feedback non-defensively. | 0 | 1 | 2 | 3 |
| 10. Reading another's non-verbal communication accurately. | 0 | 1 | 2 | 3 |
| 11. Showing empathy, identifying with another's feelings. | 0 | 1 | 2 | 3 |
| 12. Expressing my goals and intentions clearly. | 0 | 1 | 2 | 3 |
| 13. Dealing effectively with mixed messages, e.g., body says one thing, words say another. | 0 | 1 | 2 | 3 |
| 14. Remaining calm in a high stress situation. | 0 | 1 | 2 | 3 |
| 15. Giving positive feedback so that the other feels affirmed. | 0 | 1 | 2 | 3 |
| 16. Giving negative feedback appropriately. | 0 | 1 | 2 | 3 |
| 17. Coping effectively with conflict. | 0 | 1 | 2 | 3 |
| 18. Expressing feelings non-verbally and symbolically. | 0 | 1 | 2 | 3 |
| 19. Accepting others as they are. | 0 | 1 | 2 | 3 |
| 20. Describing another's behavior non-judgmentally. | 0 | 1 | 2 | 3 |
| 21. Accepting persons whose values are very unlike my own. | 0 | 1 | 2 | 3 |
| 22. Showing appreciation for the strengths of others, enjoying others. | 0 | 1 | 2 | 3 |
| 23. Checking my perceptions of another's ideas, feelings or values with them. | 0 | 1 | 2 | 3 |
| 24. Taking responsibility for meeting my own needs rather than expecting the other to meet them. | 0 | 1 | 2 | 3 |
| 25. Negotiating needs and wants (mine and another's) in an intimate relationship. | 0 | 1 | 2 | 3 |
| 26. Asking accountability of another in a relationship. | 0 | 1 | 2 | 3 |
| 27. Being accountable to another in a relationship. | 0 | 1 | 2 | 3 |
| 28. Distinguishing my feelings from my opinions. | 0 | 1 | 2 | 3 |
| 29. Expressing my own values without judging different values held by another. | 0 | 1 | 2 | 3 |
| 30. Being open to new values, attitudes, experiences. | 0 | 1 | 2 | 3 |

Take the total numerical value of the numbers you have circled and write it here.

## 3. IMAGINAL SKILLS

*Imaginal Skills:* that blend of fantasy and feeling that enables us to combine images and ideas in new ways, to see alternatives, to change conventional ways of doing things, to remedy deficiencies.

| **Skill** | **Score** |
|---|---|
| 1. The ability to "break set," i.e. to identify one's unconscious assumptions about the limits in a situation. | 0 1 2 3 |
| 2. The ability to defer judgment, to avoid the habitual response. | 0 1 2 3 |
| 3. The ability to tolerate ambiguity. | 0 1 2 3 |
| 4. The ability to daydream creatively. | 0 1 2 3 |
| 5. The ability to play with a problem, looking at it from a fresh angle, redefining it in new ways. | 0 1 2 3 |
| 6. Fluency in making fresh associations, perceiving connections or similarities between disparate realms of experience. | 0 1 2 3 |
| 7. Fluency in communicating verbally. | 0 1 2 3 |
| 8. Fluency in communicating through two-dimensional constructions, e.g., charts and graphs. | 0 1 2 3 |
| 9. Fluency in communicating in three-dimensional constructions, e.g., models. | 0 1 2 3 |
| 10. Fluency in communicating through gesture and pantomime. | 0 1 2 3 |
| 11. Fluency in communicating through movement and dance. | 0 1 2 3 |
| 12. Awareness of and sensitivity to the natural environment. | 0 1 2 3 |
| 13. Awareness of and sensitivity to the visual and tactile, to color, line, texture, composition. | 0 1 2 3 |
| 14. Awareness of and sensitivity to the auditory dimension—pitch, tone quality, rhythm, melody, harmony. | 0 1 2 3 |
| 15. Sensitivity to language, to the origins and meanings of words, ability to play with words. | 0 1 2 3 |
| 16. Fluency in communicating through poetry and drama. | 0 1 2 3 |
| 17. Trust in one's own perceptions and confidence in expressing them. | 0 1 2 3 |
| 18. Able to generate alternative solutions to problems. | 0 1 2 3 |
| 19. Able to put together existing elements or data in new ways. | 0 1 2 3 |
| 20. Able to imagine behavioral alternatives for oneself, alternative ways of expressing one's values. | 0 1 2 3 |
| 21. Able to elaborate on an idea or plan, developing the details. | 0 1 2 3 |
| 22. Able to make alternative long-term plans for oneself. | 0 1 2 3 |
| 23. Able to make alternative long-term plans for a group or organization. | 0 1 2 3 |
| 24. Able to make up stories, generate plots, tell a tale. | 0 1 2 3 |
| 25. Able to see the consequences of alternative courses of action. | 0 1 2 3 |
| 26. Able to prioritize among alternatives. | 0 1 2 3 |
| 27. Able to use brainstorming with a group to generate alternative solutions. | 0 1 2 3 |
| 28. Able to devise a variety of ways to learn in small and large groups. | 0 1 2 3 |
| 29. Able to call upon a variety of alternatives in the heat of tension or conflict situations. | 0 1 2 3 |
| 30. Able to facilitate others in generating new ideas. | 0 1 2 3 |

Take the total numerical value of the numbers you have circled and write it here.

## 4. SYSTEM SKILLS

*System Skills:* the ability to see the various parts of a system as they relate to the whole and to plan for systematic changes.

| Skill | Score |
|---|---|
| 1. Identifying the various systems at work in one's own life. | 0 1 2 3 |
| 2. Identifying a system in terms of its component parts and their functions and interactions. | 0 1 2 3 |
| 3. Distinguishing between process and content in a small group interaction. | 0 1 2 3 |
| 4. Distinguishing between process and content in large formal organizations. | 0 1 2 3 |
| 5. Distinguishing between personal and system needs in small group interactions. | 0 1 2 3 |
| 6. Distinguishing between personal and system needs in large formal organizations. | 0 1 2 3 |
| 7. Understanding one's own body as a system. | 0 1 2 3 |
| 8. Taking responsibility for one's health (being one's own doctor). | 0 1 2 3 |
| 9. Acquiring sufficient knowledge of nutrition, exercise, relaxation techniques to choose those which are best suited to oneself. | 0 1 2 3 |
| 10. Making a systems analysis of one's family. | 0 1 2 3 |
| 11. Defining one's role in one's family system. | 0 1 2 3 |
| 12. Defining one's role in one's school. | 0 1 2 3 |
| 13. Defining one's role in one's workplace. | 0 1 2 3 |
| 14. Defining one's role in one's social or friendship group or church. | 0 1 2 3 |
| 15. Ability to cope with bureaucratic paper work (license applications, registration forms, tax forms). | 0 1 2 3 |
| 16. Defining one's role in one's political grouping. | 0 1 2 3 |
| 17. Assessing the strong and weak points of one's family system. | 0 1 2 3 |
| 18. Assessing the strong and weak points of one's school. | 0 1 2 3 |
| 19. Assessing the strong and weak points of one's workplace. | 0 1 2 3 |
| 20. Assessing the strong and weak points of one's church. | 0 1 2 3 |
| 21. Assessing the strong and weak points of one's social grouping. | 0 1 2 3 |
| 22. Assessing the strong and weak points of one's political grouping (neighborhood, city, state, country, political party). | 0 1 2 3 |
| 23. Synthesizing data from a variety of sources (e.g., personal experience, statistics, interviews, research reports, emotional inputs, etc.). | 0 1 2 3 |
| 24. Ability to make sense out of apparently disparate data. | 0 1 2 3 |
| 25. Ability to organize a task, dividing it into its component parts. | 0 1 2 3 |
| 26. Ability to write job descriptions. | 0 1 2 3 |
| 27. Developing informal communication and support networks within a formal organizational system. | 0 1 2 3 |
| 28. Engaging in long-term planning and goal setting for oneself. | 0 1 2 3 |
| 29. Engaging in long-term planning and goal setting for a system of which one is a part. | 0 1 2 3 |
| 30. Communicating effectively with persons at different levels in a given system (e.g., peers, superiors, subordinates). | 0 1 2 3 |

Take the total numerical value of the numbers you have circled and write it here.

## 5. DRAWING YOUR SKILL PROFILE

Enter your four scores from this inventory in the appropriate columns in the graph below to obtain your skill profile. If you are weak in a particular area, you may want to concentrate on that section of this book and work through most of the exercises therein.

### *Your Skill Profile*

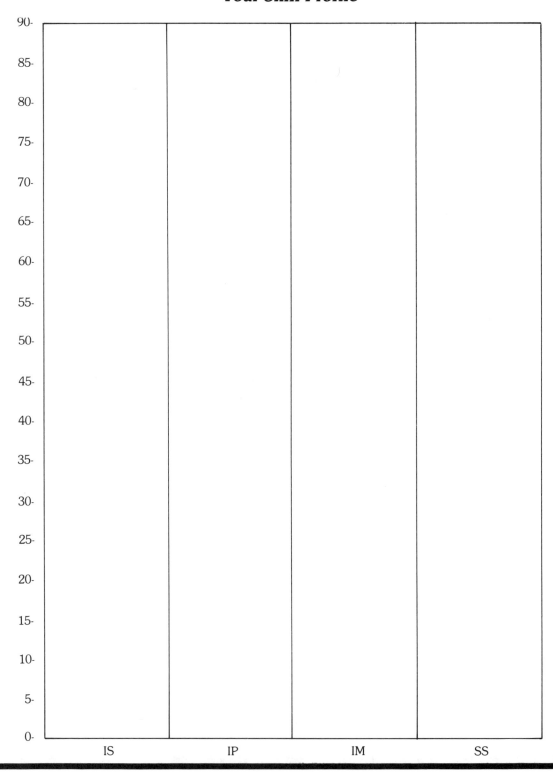

# E. Designing Your
# Personal Growth
# Contract

To make full use of the materials in this book you need to write your own unique prescription—your personal growth contract. It will enable you to identify goals and objectives that are most appropriate for your personal growth and to develop strategies to achieve them.

## 1. Primary Values and Goals

The purpose of this section is to help you to take a long-term view of your personal growth and to enable you to write a goal statement to use as a guide for the next few years.

a. List the primary values that appear in the choice section of your consciousness track.

_____

_____

_____

_____

b. Using the Values List on pages 67-68, code each primary value for the quality indicators (i.e., Work, Maintenance, Play, and Freesence as indicating the quality of the time involved). Cf. the following example:

| Value | Quality |
|-------|---------|
| Competence | W |
| Service Vocation | W |

c. Do you want these values to be important in your life three years from now? Yes____ No____

d. Does the quality coding indicate a balance of the four factors? Yes____ No ____
If you answered "no," you may want to look back at your original list of primary values and add another value or two to your list under "a" above. For instance, by adding either leisure (II B) or personal growth (III A) to the list in the example, an element of play/maintenance is introduced to balance the emphasis on work.

e. The primary values point to your over-all goals. In one or two sentences try to write a goal statement for yourself, based on your primary values.

Example: I want to decide on a career that will give me the satisfaction of serving people through my work and to develop the necessary competencies for that career. At the same time, I want to keep a good balance in my life between work and leisure.

My goal is _____

_____

_____

_____

## 2. Means Values and Objectives

The means values are just what their name implies, values that will help you achieve your goals. Means values can be translated into specific objectives, that is, observable outcomes that are measurable and achievable within a limited time frame. Such specific objectives fall within one of four categories of skills:
Instrumental
Interpersonal
Imaginal
Systems

a. List the means values that appear in the choice section of your consciousness track.

_____

_____

_____

_____

_____

b. Using the Values List on pages 67-68, code each means value with the appropriate skill category, as in the following example:

| Means Values | Skill Area |
| --- | --- |
| Achievement/success | Instrumental |
| Empathy | Interpersonal |

c. Select the two means values that are most important to you and write each as an objective. For example: Education as certification can become the following objective:

- I will achieve a GPA of 3.0 and earn my B.A. by the end of this school year.

or Self-assertion can become

- I will express both my positive and my negative feelings openly to my friends.

I will _____

_____

_____

I will _____

_____

_____

d. Identify those skills that you perceive as being most important to enable you to accomplish your objectives. You may find it helpful to refer to your skills inventory.

_____

_____

_____

_____

_____

e. You are now ready to plan strategies or ways to develop the skills you have identified, thus achieving your objectives. At this point, it is helpful to sit down with another person and brainstorm possible strategies. Cf. the following example:

*Objective:*
**To express my feelings openly**
*Strategies:*

- Use the Time Diary to get in touch with my feelings
- Share with a close friends on a fairly regular basis
- Join a personal growth group

### 3. Writing Your Personal Growth Contract
You are now ready to write your personal growth contract.

*Goals:*

1. _____

_____

2. _____

_____

*Objectives:*

1. _____

_____

2. _____

_____

*Strategies:*

1. _____

_____

2. _____

_____

3. _____

_____

4. _____

_____

5. _____

_____

6. _____

_____

*Evaluation:*

In this part of your contract identify how you will know whether or not you achieve your objectives. Many methods are available to you. You may wish to keep another diary to ascertain if there has been any change in your use of time. You may choose to utilize feedback from significant others, collect documentation, take some tests, or use any other means to determine whether change has occurred.

*Evaluation methods:*

1. ___ _____

   _____

   _____

2. _____

   _____

   _____

3. _____

   _____

   _____

*Evaluation outcomes:*

Approximately one month after setting your objectives, utilize your evaluation methods and determine your degree of success. Make changes you think are necessary and continue those strategies which are appropriate.

# List of Values

The symbols in the listing below relate each value to its appropriate place in the stages of consciousness and to the skill area associated with it. The meaning of the symbols is as follows:

**1, 2, 3, 4** name the phases of consciousness (the columns of the consciousness chart).

**A and B** indicate the two stages of each phase. The "A" stage focuses on individual values, values viewed as qualities of the person. The "B" stage focuses on values in their public and institutional aspect.

**Pr** stands for primary or ends values, those chosen for their own sake. Pr values appear at the top section of the columns.

**Me** stands for means values, those that are desired not so much for their own sake, but for what they can lead to.

IP means interpersonal skills.
IS means instrumental skills.
IM means imaginal skills.
SS means system skills.
W stands for work.
M stands for maintenance.
P stands for play.
F stands for freesence.

1. *Achievement* 2 B Me; IS; W Recognition from others for what you have done.
2. *Beauty* 3 A Pr; IM; P/F As enjoyed for its own sake.
3. *Being liked* 2 A Me; IP; M
4. *Being your own person* 3 B Pr; SS; P/M Accountable to self rather than to others.
5. *Belonging* 2 A Pr; IP; W/M Membership in a group or institution, e.g., family, church, club, corporation, etc.
6. *Building a new world* 3 B Pr; SS; W Working to change the world for the better.
7. *Candidness* 3 A Me; IP; W/M Unflinching honesty.
8. *Care and Nurturing* 2 A Me; IP; M
9. *Communication* 2 B Me; IS; W/M
10. *Companionship* 2 A Me; IP; P/M A social relationship with a person who makes me feel good about myself.
11. *Competence* 2 B Pr; IS; W
12. *Competition* 2 B Me; IS; W/M
13. *Contemplation* 3 A Pr; Is: P/F Reflection on the meaning of a thing or event.
14. *Control of others* 2 B Me; IS; M

15. *Cooperation* 3 B Me; IS; P/M
16. *Courage* 3 A Me; IP; W/M To take risks and to bear hardships to achieve what you think is right.
17. *Courtesy* 2 A Me; IP; M Politeness, good manners.
18. *Creativity* 3 B Me; IM; P
19. *Education as certification* 2 B Me; IS; W Going to school to get the degree.
20. *Education as knowledge* 3 B Me; IS; P/F Learning for its own sake.
21. *Efficiency* 2 B Me; IS; W
22. *Empathy* 3 A Me; IP; P/M To be aware of another's feelings and share in them.
23. *Equality* 3 B Me; IP; M
24. *Expressiveness* 3 A Me; IM; P/M
25. *Fairness for all* 3 B Me; SS; W/M
26. *Fate* 1 A Pr; SS; W; M
27. *Flexibility* 3 A Me; IP; P/M
28. *Generosity* 3 A Me; IP; W/M
29. *Honor* 2 B Me; SS; W/M Earning recognition by keeping the code.
30. *Human Dignity* 3 B Pr; SS; W
31. *Independence* 3 A Me; IP; P/M
32. *Initiative* 3 A Me; SS; P/M
33. *Insight* 3 B Pr; IM; P/F
34. *Interdependence* 4 A Me; SS; W
35. *Intimacy* 3 B Me; IP; P/F
36. *Law as guide* 3 A Me; SS; P/M Law not as absolute rule, but as a basis for rational decision making.
37. *Leisure* 2 B Pr; IM; P/F Time free from obligations.
38. *Living in harmony with nature* 4 B Pr; SS, P/F
39. *Living simply* 3 A Me; IS; P/M Getting along with a minimum of material things.
40. *Loyalty* 2 B Me; IP; W/M
41. *Monetary profit* 1 B Me; IS; W
42. *Mutual accountability* 3 B Me; SS, W Willingness to evaluate and to be evaluated in a peer relationship.
43. *Obeying the rules* 2 B Me; IS; W/M Law as rule.
44. *Objectivity* 2 B Me; IS; W/M Recognition of one's own bias in looking at things; separating fact from personal bias.
45. *Obligation/duty* 2 B Me; IP; W/M
46. *Orderliness* 2 A Me; IS, M Arranging time, belongings, tools, etc., in an acceptable way.
47. *Ownership of property* 2 B Me; IS; P/M
48. *Paid work* 2 B Pr; IS, M
49. *Patriotism* 2 B Me; IP; P/M

50. *Peer support/social affirmation* 2 A Me; IP; P/M Being accepted and encouraged as a member of your group.
51. *Perseverance* 3 B Me; IS; W
52. *Personal growth* 3 A Pr; IP; P/M To make an effort for self-understanding and self-development.
53. *Personal health* 3 A Me; SS; M
54. *Physical affection* 1 B Me; IP; M
55. *Physical pleasure* 1 B Me; IP; P/M
56. *Productivity* 2 B Me: IS: W
57. *Recreation/freedom* 3 B Me; 1M: P/F Time free from duties, obligations, necessary tasks, etc.
58. *Relaxation* 3 A Me: SS: P/M
59. *Risk taking* 3 B Me; IP; P
60. *Search for meaning* 3 A Me; IM; P/M
61. *Security* 1 B Pr; IP; M
62. *Self-actualization* 3 A Pr; IP; P/M The process by which the self listens to its own voice and freely chooses its path for growth.
63. *Self-assertion* 3 A Me; IP; P/M The middle ground between aggression (trampling on others) and passivity (letting others trample on oneself).
64. *Self-centeredness* 1 A Pr; IP; M
65. *Self-confidence* 2 B Pr; IS; W
66. *Self-control* 2 A Pr; IS; W
67. *Self-delight* 1 B Pr; IS; W
68. *Self-directedness* 3 A Me; IP; M

69. *Self-discipline* 3 A Me; IP; M
70. *Self-evaluation* 3 A Me; IP; M
71. *Self-preservation* 1 A Pr; IP; W/M
72. *Self-worth* 2 A Pr; IP; M
73. *Service vocation* 3 A Pr; SS; W Finding satisfaction in serving others through your work.
74. *Sexual pleasure* 1 B Me; IP; P/M
75. *Solitude* 3 B Me; SS; P/F The capacity to be at peace with oneself alone as well as with the other.
76. *Spontaneity* 3 A Pr; IM; P The ability to act with openness and immediacy.
77. *Status/rank* 2 B Me; IP; P/M
78. *Supporting your community* 3 B Me; SS; P
79. *Survival* 1 A ME;IS: M
80. *Synergy* 4 A Me; SS; P/F A process of pooling people's energies in which more creativity is generated than could result from their separate efforts.
81. *Tradition* 2 A Me; SS; P/M A sense of one's own roots.
82. *Trust* 3 A Me; IP; M
83. *Truth/wisdom* 4 A Pr; IM; P/F
84. *Wholeness* 4 A Pr; SS; P/F/M
85. *Wonder/curiosity* 1 B Me; IM; P/M Urge to know.
86. *Workmanship* 2 B Me; IS, W
87. *Worship as duty* 2 B Pr; IS; W
88. *Worship as celebration* 4 B Me; SS; P/F

# Phases and Stages of Consciousness

| | I-A | I-B | II-A | II-B | III-A | III-B | IV-A | IV-B |
|---|---|---|---|---|---|---|---|---|
| | Self-centeredness Self-preservation Fate | Security Self-delight | Belonging Self-control Self-worth | Self-confidence Competence Leisure Paid work Worship as duty | Personal growth Self-actualization Service vocation<br><br>Spontaneity | Beauty Being your own person Building a new world<br><br>Contemplation Human dignity Insight | Truth/wisdom Wholeness | Living in harmony with nature |
| | Survival | Monetary profit Physical affection Physical pleasure<br><br>Sexual pleasure Wonder/curiosity | Being liked Care and nurturing Courtesy<br><br>Companionship Orderliness<br><br>Peer support and social affirmation Tradition | Achievement Communication Competition<br><br>Control of others Education as certification Efficiency<br><br>Honor Loyalty Ownership of property Obeying rules Obligation/duty Objectivity Patriotism Productivity Status/rank Workmanship | Candidness Courage Empathy<br><br>Expressiveness Generosity Flexibility Initiative<br><br>Independence Law as guide Living simply<br><br>Personal health Relaxation Search for meaning Self-assertion Self-direction Self-discipline Self-evaluation Trust | Cooperation Creativity Education as knowledge Equality Fairness for all Intimacy Mutual accountability Perseverance Risk taking Solitude<br><br>Supporting your community Recreation/freedom | Inter-dependence Synergy | Worship as celebration |

69

# PART III: EXERCISES TO DEVELOP INSTRUMENTAL SKILLS

## Instrumental Skills

Instrumental skills are task-oriented. They are the skills that enable us to get the job done. They include the general skills needed by almost everyone in this culture, e.g., reading, writing, handling numbers; operating such appliances as a thermostat, a gas stove, an electric iron, a telephone, a television set; driving an automobile. They include all the specialized skills of business, the professions and trades, from accounting and brain surgery to plumbing. They may be cognitive—the ability to analyze an argument; or sensory-motor—the ability to ride a bicycle; or both—the ability of the artist to express an idea in line and color.

Since most of formal education is concerned with developing instrumental skills, we have made this section brief and have concentrated on a few skills that are often overlooked.

### 1. IDENTIFYING YOUR INSTRUMENTAL SKILLS

*Objectives:*
**To concretize the concept by examples.**
**To build a self-image as a competent person.**

a. Review the list of instrumental skills on page 56.
b. Make a fairly detailed list of your instrumental skills, taking into account your job or studies, your recreation and hobbies, your maintenance activities. (Cf. Time Diary.)
c. Mark your list as follows:

- "B" for the skills you are just beginning to acquire.
- "A" for those in which you are average.
- "M" for those you have mastered.
- "T" for those you are able to teach.

### 2. THE TOOLS YOU USE

A tool is any instrument one uses to accomplish a task in such a way that the user controls the form and quality of the product, e.g., a screwdriver, a power saw, a sewing machine. Instrumental skills can be viewed as the skills of using tools. At a somewhat more sophisticated level, they include the skills of designing and making tools. However, we need not think of tool-making as a highly professional activity. Workers who are fully involved in their work usually do invent short-cuts, tricks of the trade, handy helps. Any craft magazine is full of such helpful hints—not world-shaking inventions but nonetheless normal expressions of human creativity. Therefore, another way of analyzing your instrumental skills is to look at the tools you use and have made.

*Objectives:*
**To expand the analysis of your instrumental skills.**
**To build a self-image as a competent person.**

a. List the tools you have used in the last month.

- Which do you use most often?
- Which would you not have used three years ago?
- Which are you able to repair?

b. Have you ever made any tools? ever improvised a tool or made do with whatever materials and equipment happened to be on hand?
c. Did this exercise enable you to add to your list of instrumental skills?

### 3. DEVELOPING DECISION-MAKING SKILLS: CLARIFYING VALUES AND OBJECTIVES

We all make numerous decisions every day of our lives, from what to put on in the morning to which stereo to buy, which course or job to take, which friendship to develop. People vary greatly in their approaches to decision-making: some are quick and confident, others need time; some never look back, others anguish over a decision even after it is made, wondering whether they have "done the right thing." Some may be paralyzed, particularly before an important decision, hoping that circumstances will decide for them or perhaps half expecting to find an answer from heaven under the pillow when they awake in the morning. These differences are partly a matter of temperament, partly a matter of training. Often we do not realize that decision-making *is* an area for training. In fact, there are skills involved in deciding, skills that can be learned, that can help to reduce our anxieties and improve our decision-making.

A good decision is not necessarily one that turns out well; rather it is one that is well made. Among the steps that enter into a well-made decision are: clarifying values and goals, developing alternative courses of action, gathering and assessing relevant information, and assessing the consequences of the various alternatives. The process does not follow a smooth course. Seeking information about alternatives often leads to the development of new alternatives, which in turn may send you back for another look at what your priorities really are. When the decision is an important one—the choice of a major, a career, a place to live, a life partner—you may shift back and forth between the various steps several times before coming to sufficient clarity to move into action. When you feel uncertain or even paralyzed in the face of big decisions, the conscious, systematic approach can be particularly useful. This exercise and the three that follow it can help you develop some of the instrumental skills that enter into informed decision making.

*Objectives:*

**To analyze the values operative in a concrete case.**

**To identify the possible outcomes in a concrete case.**

**To relate the values to the objectives or outcomes.**

a. The concrete case: Ginny is about to graduate from the local college in Townsville with a B.A. in psychology. She is a good student, has been accepted into a graduate program in Big City, 200 miles north of Townsville. However, she is tired of class work and eager to begin working with people. Her father has died during the past year, and her mother is struggling to work part time and to maintain a home for her younger brother and sister, aged 10 and 14. She knows that her mother is depressed, and she wants to give her support, psychologically and financially. She and Hank have been seeing each other regularly and want to continue their relationship. Hank has been offered a job as a trainee with a company in Big City. It does not pay much, but the training is said to be excellent and the prospects for advancement are good. He wants Ginny to come with him to Big City. He thinks that if they get married and Ginny works part-time, they will be able to make ends meet. Ginny has been offered a job in a home for disturbed children in Townsville. It requires her to live in and the living expenses are counted as part of the modest salary. She feels torn about what to do.

b. List Ginny's possible objectives (i.e., the outcomes she desires).

c. List the values you can identify in Ginny's case. Are any of the values in conflict? (Cf. Values List on pp. 67-68.)

d. Prioritize the values according to your own views. Do these priorities determine an objective for Ginny?

e. Could you prioritize the values differently? If so, would your choice of an objective for Ginny be different?

f. Share with a partner or small group. Did others choose different priorities? different objectives?

## 4. DECISION-MAKING SKILLS: DEVELOPING AND ASSESSING ALTERNATIVES

Unless you have at least two alternatives, you have no need to make a decision, but often there are many more alternatives in a given situation than one at first realizes.

*Objectives:*

**To develop alternatives for a given situation.**

**To assess the advantages and disadvantages of each alternative.**

a. In a small group, brainstorm alternatives for Ginny and Hank. Let your imagination flow freely. Try to think the unthinkable, to let the unpleasant as well as the pleasant alternatives rise to the surface. Compare your list with ours on page 74.

b. Assess the advantages of each alternative, using the following chart:

| Alternative #1 | Probable Outcome | + or − |
|---|---|---|
| 1 | | |
| 2 | | |
| 3 | | |
| 4 | | |

Alternative #2   1 _____   _____

                    2 _____   _____

                    3 _____   _____

                    4 _____   _____

Alternative #3   1 _____   _____

                    2 _____   _____

                    3 _____   _____

                    4 _____   _____

c. What additional information would Ginny and Hank need before making a decision?

## 5. DECISION-MAKING: GATHERING AND EVALUATING INFORMATION

Gathering and evaluating information is an important part of decision-making. Reliable information can open up new alternatives and enable you to predict the outcome of a given course of action with some accuracy.

*Objectives:*
**To identify sources of information.**
**To evaluate sources of information.**

John is a college sophomore in a general liberal arts curriculum. He is thinking about declaring a major and moving toward a career choice, but feels bewildered and uncertain about where to turn.

a. What does John need to know? Here are three important sets of questions John needs to ask himself:
  (1) What am I good at? What are my present skills and aptitudes?
  (2) What do I enjoy doing? What are my interests? My likes and dislikes?
  (3) What are the career possibilities in the fields of my interest?
b. How can John find the answers to these questions?
c. How would you evaluate the reliability of the various sources?
d. Compare your answers with a partner and with the answer sheet on page 75.

## 6. DECISION-MAKING SKILLS: APPROACHES TO RISK TAKING

How much information is enough? There is no absolute answer to this question. At some point, the search for additional information becomes an evasion of the decision, and we are faced with the paradox that "not to decide is to decide." Every decision entails some risks, for we never can have all the relevant information nor can we predict accurately all the outcomes. Hence, the need for risk-taking strategies which weigh the probabilities and desirability of various outcomes against each other. It is useful to become aware of your preferred strategy, for then you will be better able to vary it to suit the situation.

*Objectives:*
**To identify various risk-taking strategies.**
**To identify your own preferred strategy.**

a. Place a waste basket in front of the room and mark three lines on the floor according to the accompanying diagram. Each member of the group chooses the line on which he or she wishes to stand and takes three turns at tossing a wad of crumpled paper into the basket.

| Participants are scored as follows: | | Basket |
|---|---|---|
| 1 for each basket from line A | _____A | 5' |
| 2 for each basket from line B | _____B | 10' |
| 4 for each basket from line C | _____C | 20' |
| The person with the highest score receives a prize. | | |

b. The two factors involved are the amount of risk and the desirability of the outcome. We can describe the three most common strategies as follows:
*High risk/high desirability:* the long shot, the wishful thinker, the gambler who is ready "to go for broke" on a slim chance.
*Low risk/low desirability:* the safe shot, for the person who wants to be sure of getting something, or, at least, of avoiding the worst. "The ship in the harbor is safe, but that's not what ships are for."
*Low to medium risk/high desirability:* a realistic strategy that tries for the best combination of desirability and probability of success.
There is a fourth possibility—*high risk/low desirability.*
At first glance, it seems unlikely that anyone would choose this strategy, but perhaps it de-

# EXERCISE 4 ANSWER SHEET

a. Some possible alternatives for Ginny, Hank, and Ginny's family:
- Ginny take a job in Townsville, Hank take job in Big City; each take a turn traveling on weekends.
- Both stay in Townsville.
- Both move to Big City; Ginny works full-time, sends money home, visits regularly.
- Everyone (including Ginny's mother and brother and sister) moves to Big City.
- Ginny and Hank either end their relationship or take a moratorium for a definite period.
- Look for a support group for Ginny's mother (friends, parents without partners, church group, women's group)

b. Advantages and disadvantages of various alternatives

| Alternative | Probable outcomes | + or − |
|---|---|---|
| (1) Gin Townsville, H in Big City | • Ginny can help mother | + |
| | • Hank starts on career ladder | + |
| | • Relationship may suffer from cost and strain of travel | − |
| (2) Both stay in Townsville | • H loses opportunity | − |
| | • G helps mother | + |
| | • H and G have time together | + |
| (3) Both move to Big City | • H takes opportunity | + |
| | • H and G have time together | + |
| | • G feels guilt about mother | − |
| | • G feels strain of travel home and sending money home | − |
| (4) Everyone moves to Big City | • G helps mother | + |
| | • H and G have time together | + |
| | • H and G have some obligation to help mother find job, living quarters | − |
| | • brother and sister have to leave friends, change schools | |
| (5) End relationship | • H starts on career ladder | + |
| | • G helps mother | + |
| | • Both H and G lose companionship, affection support | − |
| (6) G looks for support group for mother | • less strain on G | + |

74

# EXERCISE 5 ANSWER SHEET

(1) How can John find out what he is good at?
- By looking at his personal history: school grades, awards, volunteer activities.
- By taking a series of aptitude tests at the college guidance center or a career counseling center.
- By inviting feedback from his parents, friends, teachers, employers.
- By reviewing the Skills Inventory on pp. 55-59.

(2) How can John assess his interests?
- By using the Time Diary on pp. 40ff. By keeping the diary for a month and then looking at his ten best days, he will get one indicator of activities he particularly enjoys.
- By looking at what he has done with his free time in the past month.
- By dreaming about what he would do if time and money were no obstacles.
- By taking vocational and interest tests at a guidance center.

(3) How can John find out about possibilities in the fields he is interested in?
- By visiting a career guidance center for pamphlets and other materials.
- Many career guidance centers now have computerized information available. The person programs the computer according to his aptitudes and/or interests; the computer print-out reports suitable fields of work, job titles, job outlook, qualifications needed, starting salaries, possibilities of promotion, etc.
- Use the information on occupational outlook supplied by the U.S. Department of Labor. These materials are available in public and college libraries.
- By talking to practitioners in the fields of his interest.
- By getting volunteer work in the field.
- By getting an internship or a summer job in the field.
- By reading biographies of practitioners.
- By scanning journals or newsletters for people in the field.

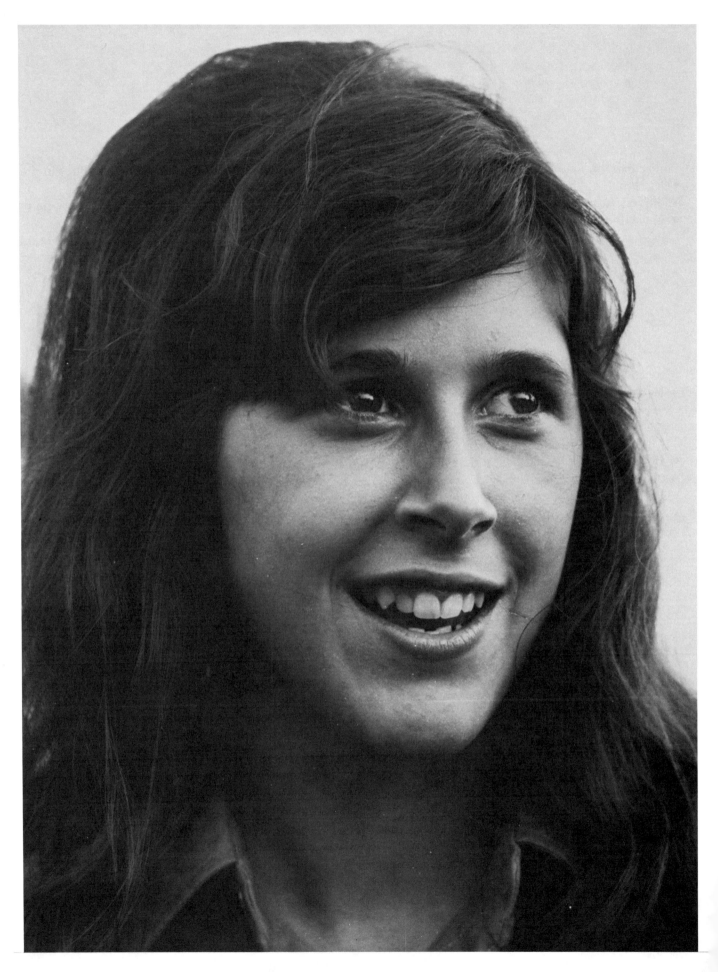

scribes the person who keeps on "hitting his or her head against a stone wall," the one who stays in an unsuitable career, risking health and psychological well-being rather than changing to something more desirable; the battered wife who remains in the marriage; the self-punishing drug addict.

   c. Think of three risks you took in the past month or two. Can you identify the strategy you used?

## 7. MORAL CHOICE AS AN INSTRUMENTAL SKILL

Modern science and technology have opened up a host of new possibilities, which in turn raise highly-charged value issues and difficult personal and public decisions. This is particularly true in the life sciences, where we are confronted with artificial insemination of human beings; sperm banks which advertise, for a price, the semen of Nobel prize winners; implantation of a fertilized human ovum in a surrogate mother; determination of the sex of the fetus; simple and safe methods of abortion; reliable but more or less risky methods of birth control; organ transplants; gene splicing capable of producing new species of living things (e.g., a bacterium that can produce insulin and another that eats up oil spills); heart, lung and kidney machines that are capable of sustaining life in a human being whose brain has ceased to function; chemicals and nuclear materials that are capable of defoliating the earth and causing cancer and genetic damage to an as yet unknown extent.

These problems elicit strong emotional responses, for they deal with matters that touch the very core of our being: birth and death, new ways of reproducing the next generation and new threats to the germ plasm, new sources of food and new ways of creating famine. Because the issues are complex, and because we can all expect to be faced with such problems either personally or as matters of public policy, we present a model for decision-making that has been developed by Jon Hendrix. It can be applied to any moral issue, enabling us to examine fully and critically the values that enter into ethical judgments and to make more confluent decisions.

## An Ethical Decision—Making Model*: Overview

1. *Identify Problem*
      a. Write a short paragraph on why you have identified your problem as a value/ethical problem for you.
      b. Use the Values List on pages 67-68 to identify and list five personal values that are expressed in your problem paragraph statement.
      c. Rank these values, from 1 = most important to you, to 5 = least important to you.
      d. Identify values in conflict.

2. List alternative solutions to problem.
3. Rank solutions by personal value preference.
4. List values or principles you hold that force you to rank a solution as #1 choice.
5. Repeat step 4 using the solution you ranked as last.
6. List consequences if your #1 ranking were implemented worldwide.
7. Assess each consequence through your "value screen" as being good (+) or bad (−).
8. Tally your assessment for step 7 and ask yourself, "Is there any 'bad' consequence(s) that overrules many 'good' consequences?"
9. Screen your #1 choice through your ethical principles; if agreement, continue to 10; if conflict, select alternate solution, i.e., #2 and repeat steps 3-9.
10. List reasons why others might not agree with your solution.
11. Place "conviction" assessment on your solution.

*Developed by Jon Hendrix

# Bioethical Decision-Making Model
## *Response Sheet*

1. Identify problem. Must be a problem that conflicts with at least two of your values, or ethical principles, and pulls you in two directions, e.g., "I ought to do *this,* but I also ought to do that." State problem as an ought to do question (e.g., What ought I do when . . .).

_____

_____

a. Write a short paragraph on why you have identified your problem as a value/ethical conflict for you.

_____

_____

_____

_____

_____

b. Use the Value List or a narrative of your values and *identify* and *list* five (5) personal values you hold that are expressed in your problem paragraph statement.

c. Ranking

1. _____

2. _____

3. _____

4. _____

5. _____

Rank these values from #1 = most important to you, to #5 = least important to you.

d. Are the number one and number two values above in conflict when you explore your problem?
Yes_____   No_____

2. List as many alternative solutions to the problem as you can, even if some do not agree with your values or principles.

Ranking                    Solutions

1. _____

2. _____

3. _____

4. _____

5. _____

6. _____

7. _____

8. _____

9. _____

10. _____

3. Rank your alternative solutions from the one (#1) your values agree with most to the one (#10) your values agree with least. (Use ranking column beside part 2.)

4. Take your *#1 solution* and list the *values/principles* you hold that cause you to rank it #1.
*#1 Solution:* (State it) _____

_____

Values/principles *you hold* that support this solution: Please try to explore at least eight values.

1. _____

2. _____

3. _____

4. _____

5. _____

6. _____

7. _____

8. _____

9. _____

10. _____

5. Take the solution you agree with *least* (ranked last) and list those values/principles you hold that cause you to rank it last.
*Last Solution:* (State it) _____

_____

Values/principles *you hold* that cause you to reject this solution: Please try to explore at least eight values.

1. _____

2. _____

3. _____

4. _____

5. _____

6. _____

7. _____

8. _____

9. _____

10. _____

6. For your #1 ranking, list as many probable consequences as you can imagine if that solution were to be implemented worldwide. *Be sure to include consequences that affect such systems as: home, family, business, government, professions, economics, psychology, medicine, law, and theology.*

Consequences
Assessment

Consequences

1. _____

2. _____

3. _____

4. _____

5. _____

6. _____

7. _____

8. _____

9. _____

10. _____

7. Place a (+) beside each consequence you hold as "good" and a (−) beside each consequence you hold as "bad." (Use column beside part 6.) Ask yourself, "Would I be willing to have this action or consequence applied to me?"

8. Tally your + and − marks. Are there any negative marks that are more important to you than the positive marks? Yes _____ No _____. If yes, star them.

9. Do you hold any ethical principles that conflict with your number one decision or its consequences? If so, list them then restate your solution or pick another solution (i.e., #2) and work through steps 3 through 9. If not, your decision is valid for you at this time in your life.

_____

10. Can you list some reasons why others may not agree with your solution?

1. _____

2. _____

3. _____

4. _____

5. _____

11. Restate your solution and place a *confidence* or *conviction* assessment on it by x-ing the number on the confidence sequence.

High                                          Low
 1 ——————— 2 ——————— 3 ——————— 4
Confidence                              Confidence

# Additional Notes on This Model

In the development of the decision-making model, the author held three basic assumptions: (1) that value/moral/ethical decision-making is developmental and confluent as exemplified in the theory of Brian Hall; (2) that the greater number of possible solutions an individual can develop and explore for a particular problem, the better the quality of decision-making; and (3) that a thorough examination of the consequences of the preferred solution will help the individual improve the quality of the decision, if the consequences are examined using systems as a frame of reference. For example, in the case of a terminally ill and comatose patient when you decide to "pull the plug," how will that decision affect the psychology (system) of the individual, the family (which is a system), law (which is a system), medicine (which also is a system)?

## The Model

The decision-making model involves the following steps. Step one is the identification of a problem or dilemma. An ethical problem is a different kind of problem. It's a problem that pulls us in two directions at once. I ought to do this, but I also ought to do that. For example, I ought to keep my husband alive, but I ought to pull the plug because he's really dead and his kidneys might save other people's lives. That is what is meant by pulling us in two different directions. The identification of a problem is followed by a short, personal narrative of why that problem is a problem for you. Students are then asked to identify the personal values in their narrative that are in conflict, and what personal values they hold concerning the problem. They are then asked to rank these values from the one that is the strongest personal value for them in their paragraph statement to the value that is the least strong. Using the Value List, they are then requested to check to see if their number one and two values are in conflict and check either a yes or a no in the space provided. For it is often the first two ranked values, the two values that they hold most strongly, that are in conflict and create the true ethical problems.

Step two on the decision-making model requires the student to list as many alternative solutions to the problem as he or she can develop. It is interesting to note that most students, when they start using the decision-making model, can only list one or two solutions. However, repeated experiences in using the model soon help individuals to generate many solutions. They begin to envision that problems have a range of solutions rather than just a "black or white" alternative. We tend to think in terms of "either-or," never considering the whole spectrum between our preferred solution and the one we abhor the most. Therefore, generating as many solutions as possible, without first thinking about their relative importance to us, becomes step two. The students then, in step three, are asked to rank their alternate solutions from the one with which their values agree most to the one with which their values agree least. Students then, in step four, take their number one ranked solution, restate it, and list the values they hold which caused them to rank it number one. They then take their last ranked solution, the one they abhor the most, and restate it and list the values they hold that caused them to rank it last (step five). This process helps students explore the full continuum of their operant values used in decision-making.

Step six involves the examination of their number one solution, but this examination now looks at the consequences incurred if their solution were to be implemented worldwide. They are asked, "What would be the consequences to certain systems such as home, family, business, government, professions, economics, psychology, medicine, law and theology if their decisions were implemented worldwide?" Students explore each of these systems very carefully and list the major consequences they can foresee if their solution were implemented on that large a scale.

Step seven involves an assessment of consequences. Students examine each of their consequences and assess them as being either positive or negative. To screen consequences, students ask themselves, "Would I be willing to have this action or consequence applied to me?" Step eight involves the tallying of all the positives and negatives; they are then asked, "Are there any positive consequences that are more important to you than the negative consequences?" Or, "Are there any negative consequences that are more important to you than the positive consequences?" If there are some negative or positive consequences that override other consequences, they are asked to star them. For often there may be one consequence of our decision with which we simply could not live, and this one negative may override many of our positive consequences. If, indeed, the students decide that they can live with the consequences, both positive and negative, of the solution, then, for them at this time in their life, the decision is an ethical one.

There are two additional steps to the decision-making model. The function of these two steps is to move the individual out of self and into the world of pluralistic values in which we live. In step ten, students are asked to list as many reasons as they can think of why other people may not agree with their solution. And finally, in step eleven, students are asked to place a confidence conviction on their solution. How confident are they in their solution? This confidence assessment, in theory, is to say to the student, "It's all right not to have absolute confidence in your solution." It's all right and, indeed, possible that tomorrow new information, new personal growth, may change the decision which we've made or may cause us to value that decision less. And not knowing that this change is about to occur is one of the limitations of our being human and is present whenever we make decisions.

But people often feel guilty once they make a critical decision and find out that the decision was a wrong one. We can, however, help students realize that we are, as human beings, limited: we do not have absolute power, absolute knowledge or absolute clarification of our values. Even thoughtful decision-making, then, will carry with it an understanding that we will make errors. This awareness of human fallibility should then go a long way to reduce the guilt reaction to a decision which, although carefully and wisely made, did not have a desired result.

# PART IV:
# EXERCISES TO DEVELOP INTERPERSONAL SKILLS

We human beings are social animals. That means that we depend on each other not only for sheer survival (think of the helplessness of the newborn infant), but also for the full development of our potentialities. Even creative geniuses in the arts or sciences cannot bring forth the new without interaction with others in their fields. A Mozart is only possible where a musical family and culture are prepared to nourish so extraordinary a talent. The lonely worker in the laboratory is using the theories and instruments developed by his or her fellow scientists and is most probably in conversation or correspondence with a chosen few colleagues. And most of us only grow into responsible, caring human beings in the supportive network of human relationships. The interpersonal skills, then, are the skills necessary to develop satisfying human relationships. They enable us to perceive ourselves and others accurately and sympathetically. They facilitate communication, mutual understanding, cooperation and intimacy.

The exercises which follow are divided into six main sections:

A. Exercises to develop *self-awareness,* since the ability to communicate with others depends first of all on knowledge of oneself.

B. Exercises to develop the communication skill of *self-disclosure,* the ability to express one's thoughts, feelings and intentions clearly.

C. Exercises to develop *active listening,* receiving messages accurately and responsively.

D. Exercises in the communication skill of giving and receiving *feedback.*

E. Exercises to develop some of the skills needed to achieve deep friendships and *intimacy.*

F. Exercises in dealing with *conflict* openly and constructively.

## A. Developing Self-Awareness

Clear communication depends upon being in touch with yourself—your own body, feelings, thoughts, intentions, actions. At any moment, a great deal is going on in us and around us. Usually, we are aware of only a small fraction of the wealth of information available about ourselves. No one can be totally self-aware all the time, but practicing brief periods of concentrated self-awareness can increase our self-knowledge and hence enable us to make better choices about what we want to become and about what we want to share with others about ourselves.

## 8. TUNING INTO YOURSELF*

*Objectives:*

**To enable participants to concentrate on the "here and now."**

**To enable participants to become more aware of their own body messages, feelings and thoughts.**

a. Find a place where you can be comfortable, maybe sitting down or stretched out on your back on the floor. Close your eyes, take a few deep breaths and exhale slowly.

b. Pay attention to your own awareness. Say to yourself, "Now I am aware of. . . ." Try to focus your awareness on this instant. Notice where your awareness goes. Is it going to something inside your skin or to something outside it?

c. Turn outside. What are your senses telling you about the here and now? What do you hear? smell? taste? Open your eyes—what do you see? What are you touching? How does it feel on your skin? Are you aware of the points where your body is touching the chair or the floor?

d. Focus on your body. Which parts come immediately into awareness? Which parts do not give a clear sensation even when you focus on them? Try focusing on one part of your body at a time and tensing and relaxing just that part, e.g., the toes on your left foot, your left ankle, left calf, left knee; then do the same for your right foot, etc.

---

*Adapted from John O. Stevens, *Awareness, Exploring, Experimenting, Experiencing.* Real People Press, Moab, Utah, 1971.

e. Now notice your feelings. A good place to begin is with the physical sensations in your body that usually accompany feelings, e.g., sweating, dry mouth, tense muscles, smiling, butterflies in your stomach, rapid heartbeat, etc. Are you feeling excited, anxious, bored or whatever?

f. Now pay attention to your thoughts—the stream of ideas, beliefs, memories, plans, assumptions, evaluations, interpretations that pass through your mind.

g. Pair and share with a partner:

- How did you feel during this exercise?
- Did you make any discoveries about yourself?
- Were you able to stay in the here and now?
- Have you ever practiced any kind of centering exercise before—e.g. hatha yoga, TM, Quaker silent worship, Christian meditation?

## 9. USING THE AWARENESS WHEEL*

*Objectives:*

**To increase awareness of the amount of data available to the self about the self at any given moment.**

**To enable one to distinguish clearly between sensory impressions, thoughts, feelings, intentions and actions.**

a. Below is a diagram and explanation of the "Awareness Wheel." After reading it, fill out Work Sheet Ex. 9.

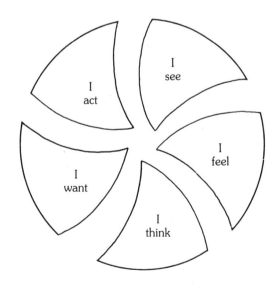

The awareness wheel is a helpful device for bringing more of our moment-to-moment experience into full

awareness. Practicing with the awareness wheel is an important step in learning to send clear messages, for we can only verbalize what is within the focus of our conscious attention. Often we may have conflicting intentions or mixed feelings; in that case, tapping into the awareness wheel can be both a clarifying and a freeing experience.

"*I see*" refers to direct sensory experience, the immediate data supplied by eyes, ears, nose, taste, touch.

"*I think*" expresses an opinion, idea, belief, assumption, interpretation, evaluation, expectation or conclusion. "I see that you are frowning and I think I've done something to offend you." Actually, you have a headache. It is important to keep in mind that alternative interpretations are always possible, and that two people often come to very different interpretations of the same sense data.

"*I feel*" refers to being pleased, uncomfortable, irritated, elated, bored, or whatever. See the list of feeling words on page 86. Note that feelings can always be expressed by "I feel" followed by an adjective.

"*I want*" states my goal, aim or intention, i.e., what I want for myself in this situation. Often we fail to make our intentions clear either because we are unaware of them, or because we think they are either obvious or unimportant, or because we want to keep them hidden (e.g., "I want you to admire me"). Sometimes intentions get expressed indirectly as "shoulds," e.g., "You should finish that job" instead of "I would like you to. . . ."

"*I act*" names my behavior. I may think I know what I am doing, but actually I am usually aware of only part of my behavior. My facial expressions, posture, tone of voice, and habitual gestures may be outside the focus of my attention and may be sending strong messages that interfere with my verbal communication.

b. Find a partner and compare notes on Work Sheet Ex. 9. If you are working with a group, enter a general discussion to clarify any questions or disagreements. Our interpretation of the exercise is on sheet Ex. 9a.

c. Take five minutes in silence to run through the awareness wheel for yourself, starting wherever you wish, and jot down your impressions.

d. Questions for reflection and discussion:

- What came to you first? Most of us are more in touch with some parts of the wheel than with others. If you know this about yourself, you can increase your self-awareness by conscious attention to the other parts of the wheel.
- What difficulties did you experience in using the wheel?
- Did you discover anything about yourself?

---

*Adapted from Miller, Nunnally, & Wackman, *Alive and Aware.* Interpersonal Communication Programs, Inc., Minneapolis, 1975.

# WORK SHEET EX. 9

## Moving Around the Awareness Wheel

In the fifteen statements below, one of the five dimensions of the awareness wheel is represented. Next to each statement, indicate the dimension, using the following letters:

(s) - sensing
(t) - thinking
(f) - feeling
(i) - wanting
(a) - acting

1. You don't even care how I feel about it.                                      1. _____
2. I'm depressed because I didn't get the job.                                   2. _____
3. My boss is a real jerk.                                                        3. _____
4. I see that you are upset.                                                      4. _____
5. I really don't feel like going to the dance tonight.                          5. _____
6. I'm so excited—John just called me.                                           6. _____
7. I'm listening.                                                                7. _____
8. I'll take care of it the first thing tomorrow.                                8. _____
9. Last night at dinner, I heard you say you wanted to see that show.            9. _____
10. I stopped at the bank on the way home today.                                 10. _____
11. I smell something good on the stove.                                         11. _____
12. I'm a failure—I'll never amount to anything.                                 12. _____
13. I'm really afraid to try.                                                     13. _____
14. I'd like to tell you how I'm feeling about our relationship.                 14. _____
15. I felt a cool breeze on my face.                                             15. _____

# ANSWER SHEET: EX. 9

1. t
2. f
3. t   (My opinion, or evaluation, probably with anger or resentment behind it.)
4. t   (My interpretation—I *see* tears, hear a shaky voice, see trembling hands, and infer "upset.")
5. i   (Not a feeling but a desire—I want not to go.)
6. f
7. a   (I am actively attending to you.)
8. i   (my intention)
9. s
10. a
11. s
12. t   (My opinion or conclusion, which may or may not be based on solid evidence.)
13. f
14. i
15. s

## List of Feeling Words
(Taken from Marshall B. Rosenberg's book *From Now On*)
# NEGATIVE

| | | | | |
|---|---|---|---|---|
| afraid | chagrined | dissatisfied | hesitant | lethargy |
| aggravated | cold | distant | horrified | listless |
| agitation | concerned | distressed | horrible | lonely |
| alarm | confused | disturbed | hostile | mad |
| aloof | cool | down | hot | mean |
| angry | cross | embittered | humdrum | melancholy |
| anguish | credulous | exasperated | hurt | miserable |
| animosity | critical | exhausted | impatient | mopy |
| annoyance | dejected | fatigued | indifferent | pessimistic |
| anxious | depressed | fearful | inert | pissed off |
| apathetic | despair | fidgety | infuriated | provoked |
| apprehensive | despondent | flaky | insecure | puzzled |
| aversion | detached | forlorn | insensitive | rattled |
| bad | disappointed | frightened | intense | reluctant |
| beat | discouraged | frustrated | irate | repelled |
| bitter | disgruntled | furious | irked | resentful |
| blah | disgusted | gloomy | irritated | restless |
| blown up | disheartened | grief | jealous | sad |
| blue | disinterested | grumpy | jittery | scared |
| bored | dislike | guilty | keyed-up | sensitive |
| burned up | dismayed | hate | lassitude | shaky |
| breathless | displeased | heavy | lazy | shocked |
| brokenhearted | disquieted | helpless | let down | skeptical |
| sleepy | surprised | troubled | unhappy | weary |
| sorrowful | suspicion | uncomfortable | unnerved | withdrawn |
| sorry | tepid | unconcerned | unsteady | woeful |
| sour | terrified | uneasy | upset | worried |
| spiritless | thwarted | unglued | uptight | wretched |
| startled | tired | | | |

## List of Feeling Words
(Taken from Marshall B. Rosenberg's book *From Now On*)
# POSITIVE

| | | | | |
|---|---|---|---|---|
| absorbed | dazzled | groovy | pleasant |
| adventurous | delighted | happy | proud |
| affectionate | eager | helpful | quiet |
| alert | ecstatic | hopeful | radiant |
| alive | elated | inquisitive | refreshed |
| amazed | electrified | inspired | relieved |
| amused | encouraged | intense | satisfied |
| animated | engrossed | interested | secure |
| appreciative | enjoyment | intrigued | sensitive |
| astonished | enlivened | invigorated | spellbound |
| blissful | enthusiastic | involved | splendid |
| breathless | exalted | joyful | stimulated |
| buoyant | excited | jubilant | surprised |
| calm | exhilarated | keyed up | tender |
| carefree | expansive | loving | tenderness |
| cheerful | expectant | mellow | thankful |
| comfortable | exuberant | merry | thrilled |
| composed | fascinated | mirthful | touched |
| concerned | free | moved | tranquil |
| confident | friendly | optimistic | trusting |
| contented | fulfilled | overwhelmed | warm |
| cool | good-humored | overjoyed | wide-awake |
| curious | grateful | peaceful | |

## 10. AUTOMATIC WRITING

*Objectives:*

**To increase self-awareness and personal insight.**

**To encourage free association as a means of getting in touch with concerns that are below conscious awareness.**

a. Choose a stimulus phrase from the list below and write for five to ten minutes, without lifting pen from paper. Just write down whatever comes to mind, regardless of whether it relates to the stimulus phrase, and without worrying about grammar or spelling. Generally, the more quickly the words are written, the better. Either set an alarm clock to ring at the end of the pre-arranged time, or, if you are working in a group, appoint a timekeeper, so that you need not distract yourself by looking at a clock.

b. Repeat once or twice more.

c. Read what you have written. Are you aware of your "internal censor" that might have worried about sharing or even writing down some of these thoughts? Can you get in touch with some of your concerns about taking risks?

d. Choose someone you would like to get to know better and exchange writings. What do you perceive in the other's writing? What does he or she see in yours? Do you feel differently toward each other as a result of this exercise?

e. Choose someone you are already acquainted with and exchange writings with him or her. Did you open up any deeper channels of communication?

f. Role play your internal censor with your partner in (d) or (e) above taking the part of yourself. How strong is your censor? Did you gain any new insights into your self and your willingness to risk?

**Suggested Stimulus Phrases**

Who am I?
Who really knows me?
I am presently aware that . . .
My weakest point is . . .
When I think about the future, I feel . . .
My greatest fear is . . .
I am happiest when . . .
My strongest point is . . .
I feel most affectionate when . . .

## 11. GETTING IN TOUCH WITH THE OTHER SIDE OF YOUR MIND

In recent years, science has become aware that each of us has not one, but two brains, the left hemisphere and the right hemisphere. For right-handed people, the left hemisphere is dominant and contains speech, ideas, facts, concepts and thinking. The right hemisphere contains the symbolic, the intuitive, the imaginative and emotive (feelings). Because our feelings are often in the non-cognitive hemisphere, it is often difficult to get in touch with them. This exercise will enable you to become aware of how your non-dominant hemisphere feels about yourself by allowing it to express itself through your non-dominant hand, "the hand you don't write with."

*Objective:*

**To better understand yourself by becoming more aware of the non-dominant hemisphere of your brain.**

a. Draw a picture of yourself with the hand you normally write with. The picture should include your whole body and contain as much detail as you can draw in five (5) minutes. Label this "Picture A."

b. Set the picture aside and draw another picture of yourself with your other hand. The picture should include your whole body and contain as much detail as you can draw in five (5) minutes. Label this "Picture B."

c. Find a partner. Set the pictures side by side and ask your partner to compare them in regard to the following points: Which picture looks
younger
more relaxed
more alive
happier
more compassionate
more loving
more confident
more attractive
more sexual
more open
more alert
more intelligent
more energetic
more competent

d. Look at your partner's pictures and respond to them in terms of the above points. Write ten words on each of your partner's pictures, using Rosenberg's list of feeling words on pp. 86.

e. Look at the list of words on your two pictures. Picture "A" indicates how you "think" you are and how you try to present yourself to others. Picture "B" indicates how you really feel about yourself.

f. Do you agree with your partner's judgments? If not, which words would you select to describe each picture?

g. In which picture do you like yourself better? Why?

## 12. BECOMING AWARE OF YOUR "SELF-TALK"

Most of us carry on an internal dialogue with ourselves most of the time. This "self-talk" is usually sending us messages at an almost subliminal level, messages which may be either congratulatory or condemnatory: "I handled that pretty well." "I look terrible." Turning the full light of consciousness on our self-talk enables us to test our assumptions against reality. It is particularly useful to do this when dealing with negative feelings about ourselves. Before doing these exercises, read chapters 10 and 11, in *Readings in Value Development*.

*Objectives:*

**To become aware of self-talk.**

**To identify underlying assumptions of self-talk.**

**To evaluate these underlying assumptions.**

**To practice new self-talk.**

a. Get comfortable, center down, and turn your attention inward. Think of a specific time when you felt sad, disappointed or depressed. Use Work Sheet Ex. 12 to help you imagine the situation in detail.

b. Jot down your self-talk in the situation.

c. Analyze the assumptions underlying your self-talk, using the list on the exercise sheet and any other assumptions that occur to you.

d. Look at the assumptions you have identified. Which ones do you agree with? Disagree with?

e. Reformulate the assumptions you disagree with into statements you can make with conviction, e.g.,

- I do not have to be perfect.
- My early childhood experiences do not irrevocably determine my behavior; I can do something about changing my behavior.

f. Make a plan for practicing your new statement(s). Practice can include:

- taking a few minutes at the beginning and end of the day to repeat the new statement to yourself;
- jotting your statement on a card or slip of paper and putting it where you will be sure to see it every day;
- keeping a personal journal for a few weeks in which you note down your efforts to change your self-talk and their results.

## 13. GETTING IN TOUCH WITH YOUR "CORE SELF"

*Objectives:*

**To enable participants to become aware of "the one" and "the many" within themselves.**

**To enable participants to get in touch with the core self sufficiently to be able to act from it.**

a. Read Chapter 12 in *Readings in Value Development* on "The Higher Consciousness," especially the first fourteen pages which distinguish the "core self" from the clamorous crowd of sub-personalities or "small" I's.

b. Think of a decision which you made in good faith but then were unable to carry out—perhaps you decided to get up early and jog every day, or to lose five pounds, or to spend more time in study, or to stop smoking.

c. Close your eyes and imagine the situation in detail, as in exercise 12 above: Where were you? What time of day was it? Who else was there? As you feel your way back into the time of decision, try to hear what your various "small I's" were saying. Use the phrase, "Part of me is saying (or is feeling). . . ."

d. Jot down what you hear the different voices within you saying. Can you now get in touch with the core self which is not identical with any of the "small I's"? Can you now make a more realistic decision, one which takes into account and harmonizes the various voices within?

## 14. DISTINGUISHING THOUGHTS AND FEELINGS

Many of us have too small a vocabulary of feeling words to do justice to the complexity and richness of our feelings. Moreover, we may have the common American habit of saying "I feel" when we intend to express a thought or an opinion rather than a feeling.

*Objectives:*

**To heighten awareness of the difference between thoughts and feelings.**

**To increase participants' vocabulary of feeling words.**

**To enable participants to describe their own feelings in non-judgmental language.**

a. Participants are asked to close their eyes and to imagine the fantasy situation, illustrated in "b" below, as vividly and in as much detail as possible.

b. Facilitator describes situation:

*Fantasy:* Imagine that you are on a picnic in the country and are caught in a thunderstorm. The sky darkens,

## WORKSHEET EX. 12

### Getting In Touch With My Self-Talk

Think of a specific situation when you had some negative feeling—sadness, disappointment, anxiety, depression.

Use the following questions to help you imagine as concretely as possible the specific situation:

- Where was I? What did the place look like?
- When was it? What time of day?
- What was I wearing?
- Who was there?

- Whom was I interacting with?
- What is our relationship?
- What did I say/do?
- What did the other say/do
- How did I feel?

What was I saying to myself? Was I saying any of the following?

- I'm dumb.
- It was all my fault.
- . . . doesn't like me.
- other (jot down)

- I fouled up.
- I'll never be able to do . . .
- It'll be a disaster if . . . happens.

Look at what you have written above. What assumptions are you making? Are you assuming any of the following?

- I should be thoroughly competent and achieving in all respects.
- Everyone I meet should like me.

- It's terrible if things don't go the way I'd like.
- Unhappiness is externally caused, and I cannot do anything about it.

- My feelings are too strong to be controlled.

- I have a right to be dependent; there should be somebody strong enough to take care of me.
- My early childhood experiences determine my feelings and behavior so I can't change.
- It is easier to avoid difficulties than to face them.
- There is invariably one right solution in every situation and it is terrible if it isn't found.

Do I agree with my assumptions stated above? If not, how would I change them?

the wind blows more strongly. You hear the rumbles of distant thunder and hastily start to gather up your belongings. The lightning flashes light up heavy masses of black clouds. Slowly the rain begins, until it becomes a steady downpour. Feel the raindrops hitting you. The lightning hits a tree near you, ripping off a limb. The wind lashes the tree tops and bites through your clothes. You can hardly manage to walk against it. You smell the air and the wet earth, as you struggle toward your car. Suddenly, the storm ends and the sun appears.

c. What are you aware of right now as the fantasy mood ends? Jot down your responses; then go around the circle, sharing your statements.

d. Discuss:

* Did people tend to answer more with feelings, thoughts, or descriptive statements?
* If you answered with thoughts or descriptions, what were your feelings?
* Does your answer tell you anything about yourself?

e. Group can now brainstorm and list on newsprint all the feeling words mentioned in the above discussion. Then break into small groups of three or four and brainstorm additional feeling words. Compare the list with the List of Feeling Words on pp. 67. The group may want to spend some time discussing the shades of meaning conveyed by some of the words they do not ordinarily use.

*Note: An Alternative Fantasy*

Imagine that you are walking down a country road on a hot, sunny day. The road is dusty, and you breathe in some of the dust. You pass an abandoned house, the windows broken and the door hanging by one hinge. You come to a covered bridge. It is a long, dark tunnel—you cannot see the light at the other end. It smells damp and musty. A spider web brushes across your face. Your footsteps echo in the darkness. You can hear the water of the creek rushing beneath you. Suddenly you step on a rotten board and your foot goes through. You catch a glimpse of rocks and dark water beneath you. You grab a post and haul your foot back up, scratching your leg on the broken board. You begin to run, gasping for breath, hardly able to breathe the dead musty air. Finally, you see the light and stumble out onto a grassy bank in the sunshine.

## 15. IDENTIFYING FEELING STATEMENTS

*Objectives:*

**To distinguish clear from unclear expressions of feelings.**

**To revise mixed or unclear statements in order to make them clear statements of feelings.**

a. Participants fill out work sheet Ex. 15.
b. Pair with partner and discuss.
c. Discuss disagreements in total group.

* Note that the words "I feel that" always introduce a thought or opinion. Feelings are facts and do not admit of argument. But opinions are interpretations; my interpretation can differ from yours, and there is room for argument. Introducing an opinion under the cover of "I feel" often effectively stifles disagreement, or at least makes free discussion more difficult.
* Note that some feeling words contain overtones of blaming—"I feel put down, or ripped off, or ignored." Such words imply that the other is at fault, and will therefore provoke defensiveness. Try to express your own feelings without blaming anyone else.

d. Review the sentences that state opinions rather than feelings. Rewrite them to make them clear statements of feelings and share in the total group.

## 16. A FANTASY TRIP*

*Objective:*

**To encourage free association as a means of getting in touch with concerns below the level of conscious awareness.**

a. Find a comfortable position for writing; close your eyes; center down; take a few slow, deep breaths.
b. Think of yourself as a bird. What kind of a bird would you like to be? Let your imagination range freely and write a story about the bird.
c. Reread your story in the light of the following questions:

* Is the bird large or small? brightly colored or neutral?
* Is the bird ordinary or rare and exotic?
* Where does it live? caged or free? in pleasant or in harsh surroundings?
* Is it alone or with others of its kind?
* Are the others friendly?
* Are there enemies lurking about, seeking to trap or kill the bird?
* How does the bird spend its days?

d. Does your story tell you anything about yourself? about how you see the world? about your relationships?

---

*Adapted from Andrew Panzarella, *Microcosm*. St. Mary's College Press, Winona, Minn., 1972.

# WORK SHEET EX. 15

## Expressing Feelings

Put a check mark next to each of the following statements which clearly expresses the speaker's feelings. Then try to rewrite the others.

1. I feel you are the most selfish person I've ever met.
2. We all feel you're a wonderful person.
3. I feel put down.
4. I'm really angry that you were so late for dinner.
5. I feel we should focus on finding a way to fight the increase in nuclear power plants.
6. I feel misunderstood.
7. Can't you see I'm busy?
8. I feel that you are really inaccessible.
9. I feel that you're being unfair.
10. I felt upset when you interrupted my story at the dinner last night.

*Note:* If the group has built an atmosphere of openness and trust, you may wish to pair off and exchange stories and interpretations with a partner.

## 17. EXPLORING THE UNKNOWN
*Objective:*

**To increase participants' awareness of their reluctance to take risks, to venture into the unknown.**

*Resources:*
Someone to act as a facilitator and three others to act as assistants. Blindfolds for all but three of the participants. Check sheets for observers. (Cf. Work Sheet Ex. 17.)

a. The group agrees on the selection of a facilitator and three assistants who will act as observers.
b. The facilitator and the assistants then blindfold the other participants. Both facilitators and assistants should remain silent from this point. When all have been blindfolded, the observers take their stand in a nearby room. The facilitator then leads each participant into that room, turns him or her around several times and then lets him or her go.
c. Observers note behaviors on their check sheets.
d. After five or ten minutes, facilitator calls time and opens a discussion:

- How did individuals experience themselves in this situation?
- How much did they move about?
- What did they hold on to?
- How did they feel?
- Observers then feed back what they noticed.

e. Does this tell you anything about how you behave in a new and unfamiliar situation? about your willingness to take risks?

## 18. ACCEPTING ONESELF
This exercise has been designed to help you make some discoveries about yourself. To be able to grow and to make full use of your powers, it is very important to accept all the parts of your self. There may be some parts you do not like, or perhaps that you are even ashamed of. It is possible to change these, but only if you begin by accepting all of yourself as you are here and now, with your strengths and limitations, positive and negative feelings, successes and failures.

You may remember the story of the little boy who blurted out during the royal parade, "But the emperor has no clothes on!" He is a good model for self-acceptance. Self-acceptance involves at a minimum:

1. seeing what is actually there instead of what is supposed to be there, or was once there, or what we would like to see there;
2. feeling what you feel, and naming what you feel, not what you are expected to feel.

The further step of self-assertion involves saying what *you* see, think or feel, rather than what others expect you to say. This is easier to do in proportion to the degree of openness and mutual trust present in the communications climate.
*Objective:*

**To encourage participants to accept their total selves.**

a. A Personal Reflection
   1. Center down.
   2. Reflect on your feelings.

   - How do you treat your feelings?
   - Do you let yourself become aware of what you really feel? even when it may be negative? or upsetting? or frightening?
   - Do you ever pretend to have feelings you don't have?
   - Do you ever try to cover up feelings which you would prefer not to have?

b. Practicing Self-Affirmation

   1. Divide into groups of six or eight persons.
   2. Take a few moments for each person to think of something he or she does well and takes pride in.
   3. Participants arrange themselves in a line, one behind the other. The first person turns toward the second and says as confidently as possible, "I am a competent. . . ." The others check for eye contact, tone of voice, nervous laughter or gestures. The second person turns to the third, and so on down the line until each has had a turn.
   4. Discuss:

   - How did you feel?
   - What do you think the non-verbals indicate?
   - Why is it so difficult to state a personal strength in a simple, direct way?

## 19. IDENTIFYING ONE'S PERSONALITY TYPE
There are many typologies available for understanding different types of personality. One useful typology, discussed in Chapter 11 of *Readings in Value Development,* is based on the Jungian classification of thinking/feeling, intuitive/sensate, extravert/introvert,

## OBSERVERS CHECK SHEET: EX. 17

*Note:* Observers may wish to divide the group among themselves, so that each observer watches only four or five people.

| | A | B | C | D | E |
|---|---|---|---|---|---|
| 1. Did anyone refuse to move, stand rooted to the spot? | | | | | |
| 2. Did anyone sit down on the floor? | | | | | |
| 3. How did people move? | | | | | |
| 4. Did anyone touch another person and cling to him or her? | | | | | |
| 5. Did anyone touch another and then let go of him or her? | | | | | |
| 6. Did anyone find a wall or pillar and stay with it? | | | | | |
| 7. What sounds did people make? any giggles or nervous laughter? | | | | | |
| 8. Did anyone keep moving, exploring the space? | | | | | |
| 9. Did the behavior change in the course of the exercise? If so, how? | | | | | |

structure/flow (or, in the terms used in the following Inventory, judging/perceiving). The following Personal Style Inventory will enable you to place yourself on these dimensions.

*Objectives:*

**To use the Personal Style Inventory.**

**To check one's self knowledge against the instrument.**

  a. Fill out the inventory.
  b. Read the description of the different types as set forth in chapter 11.
  c. Make a prediction of your personality type: Do you think you tend more toward T or F, N or S, E or I, J or P?
  d. Score your test and compare the result with your prediction.
  e. Check your score with someone who knows you well. Does he or she agree with the test results?
  f. List for yourself the advantages and disadvantages of your typology.

## PERSONAL STYLE INVENTORY INTERPRETATION SHEET

Letters on the score sheet stand for:

I - introversion        E - extroversion
N - intuition           S - sensing
T - thinking            F - feeling
P - perceiving          J - judging

If your score is: the likely interpretation is:

20–21  balance in the strengths of the dimensions

22–24  some strength in the dimension; some weakness in the other member of the pair

25–29  definite strength in the dimension; definite weakness in the other member of the pair

30–40  considerable strength in the dimension; considerable weakness in the other member of the pair

Your typology is those four dimensions for which you had scores of 22 or more, although the relative strengths of all the dimensions actually constitute your typology. Scores of 20 or 21 show relative balance in a pair so that either member could be part of the typology.

## DIMENSIONS OF THE TYPOLOGY

The following four pairs of dimensions are present to some degree in all people. It is the extremes that are described here. The strength of a dimension is indicat-ed by the score for that dimension and will determine how closely the strengths and weaknesses described fit the participant's personality.

### Introversion—Extroversion

Persons more introverted than extroverted tend to make decisions somewhat independently of constraints and prodding from the situation, culture, people, or things around them. They are quiet, diligent at working alone, and socially reserved. They may dislike being interrupted while working and may tend to forget names and faces.

Extroverted persons are attuned to the culture, people, and things around them, endeavoring to make decisions congruent with demands and expectations. The extrovert is outgoing, socially free, interested in variety and in working with people. The extrovert may become impatient with long, slow tasks and does not mind being interrupted by people.

### Intuition—Sensing

The intuitive person prefers possibilities, theories, gestalts, the overall, invention, and the new and becomes bored with nitty-gritty details, the concrete and actual, and facts unrelated to concepts. The intuitive person thinks and discusses in spontaneous leaps of intuition that may leave out or neglect details. Problem solving comes easily for this individual, although there may be a tendency to make errors of fact.

The sensing type prefers the concrete, real, factual, structured, tangible here-and-now, becoming impatient with theory and the abstract, mistrusting intuition. The sensing type thinks in careful, detail-by-detail accuracy, remembering real facts, making few errors of fact, but possibly missing a conception of the overall.

### Feeling—Thinking

The feeler makes judgments about life, people, occurrences, and things based on empathy, warmth, and personal values. As a consequence, feelers are more interested in people and feelings than in impersonal logic, analysis, and things, and in conciliation and harmony more than in being on top or achieving impersonal goals. The feeler gets along well with people in general.

The thinker makes judgments about life, people, occurrences, and things based on logic, analysis, and evidence, avoiding the irrationality of making decisions based on feelings and values. As a result, the thinker is more interested in logic, analysis, and verifiable conclusions than in empathy, values, and personal warmth. The thinker may step on others' feelings and needs without realizing it, neglecting to take into consideration the values of others. (Con't. on p. 98.)

# PERSONAL STYLE INVENTORY*

Just as every person has differently shaped feet and toes from every other person, so we all have differently "shaped" personalities. Just as no person's foot shape is "right" or "wrong," so no person's personality shape is right or wrong. The purpose of this inventory is to give you a picture of the shape of your preferences, but that shape, while different from the shapes of other persons' personalities, has nothing to do with mental health or mental problems.

The following items are arranged in pairs (a and b), and each member of the pair represents a preference you may or may not hold. Rate your preference for each item by giving it a score of 0 to 5 (0 meaning you *really* feel negative about it or strongly about the other member of the pair, 5 meaning you *strongly* prefer it or do not prefer the other member of the pair). The scores for a and b MUST ADD UP TO 5 (0 and 5, 1 and 4, 2 and 3, etc.). *Do not use fractions such as 2½.*

I prefer:

1a. _____ making decisions after finding out what others think.
 b. _____ making decisions without consulting others.

2a. _____ being called imaginative or intuitive.
 b. _____ being called factual and accurate.

3a. _____ making decisions about people in organizations based on available data and systematic analysis of situations.
 b. _____ making decisions about people in organizations based on empathy, feelings, and understanding of their needs and values.

4a. _____ allowing commitments to occur if others want to make them.
 b. _____ pushing for definite commitments to ensure that they are made.

5a. _____ quiet, thoughtful time alone.
 b. _____ active, energetic time with people.

6a. _____ using methods I know well that are effective to get the job done.
 b. _____ trying to think of new methods of doing tasks when confronted with them.

7a. _____ drawing conclusions based on unemotional logic and careful step-by-step analysis.
 b. _____ drawing conclusions based on what I feel and believe about life and people from past experiences.

8a. _____ avoiding making deadlines.
 b. _____ setting a schedule and sticking to it.

9a. _____ talking a while and then thinking to myself about the subject.
 b. _____ talking freely for an extended period and thinking to myself at a later time.

10a. _____ thinking about possibilities.
 b. _____ dealing with actualities.

11a. _____ being thought of as a thinking person.

11b. _____ being thought of as a feeling person.
12a. _____ considering every possible angle for a long time before and after making a decision.
12b. _____ getting the information I need, considering it for a while, and then making a fairly quick, firm decision.
13a. _____ inner thoughts and feelings other cannot see.
13b. _____ activities and occurrences in which others join.
14a. _____ the abstract or theoretical.
14b. _____ the concrete or real.
15a. _____ helping others explore their feelings.
15b. _____ helping others make logical decisions.
16a. _____ change and keeping options open.
16b. _____ predictability and knowing in advance.
17a. _____ communicating little of my inner thinking and feelings.
17b. _____ communicating freely my inner thinking and feelings.
18a. _____ possible views of the whole.
18b. _____ the factual details available.
19a. _____ using common sense and conviction to make decisions.
19b. _____ using data, analysis, and reason to make decisions.
20a. _____ planning ahead based on projections.
20b. _____ planning as necessities arise, just before carrying out the plans.
21a. _____ meeting new people.
21b. _____ being alone or with one person I know well.
22a. _____ ideas.
22b. _____ facts.
23a _____ convictions.
23b. _____ verifiable conclusions.
24a. _____ keeping appointments and notes about commitments in notebooks or in appointment books as much as possible.
24b. _____ using appointment books and notebooks minimally as possible (although I may use them).
25a. _____ discussing a new, unconsidered issue at length in a group.
25b. _____ puzzling out issues in my mind, then sharing the results with another person.
26a. _____ carrying out carefully laid, detailed plans with precision.
26b. _____ designing plans and structures without necessarily carrying them out.
27a. _____ logical people.
27b. _____ feeling people.
28a. _____ being free to do things on the spur of the moment.
28b. _____ knowing well in advance what I am expected to do.
29a. _____ being the center of attention.
29b. _____ being reserved.
30a. _____ imagining the non-existent.
30b. _____ examining details of the actual.
31a. _____ experiencing emotional situations, discussions, movies.
31b. _____ using my ability to analyze situations.
32a. _____ starting meetings at a pre-arranged time.
32b. _____ starting meetings when all are comfortable or ready.

# PERSONAL STYLE INVENTORY SCORING SHEET

*Instructions:* Transfer your scores for each item of each pair to the appropriate blanks. Be careful to check the a and b letters to be sure you are recording scores in the right blank spaces. Then total the scores for each dimension.

## Dimension

| I | E | N | S |
|---|---|---|---|
| **Item** | **Item** | **Item** | **Item** |
| 1b. _____ | 1a. _____ | 2a. _____ | 2b. _____ |
| 5a. _____ | 5b. _____ | 6b. _____ | 6a. _____ |
| 9a. _____ | 9b. _____ | 10a. _____ | 10b. _____ |
| 13a. _____ | 13b. _____ | 14a. _____ | 14b. _____ |
| 17a. _____ | 17b. _____ | 18a. _____ | 18b. _____ |
| 21b. _____ | 21a. _____ | 22a. _____ | 22b. _____ |
| 25b. _____ | 25a. _____ | 26b. _____ | 26a. _____ |
| 29b. _____ | 29a. _____ | 30a. _____ | 30b. _____ |
| TOTAL I_____ | TOTAL E_____ | TOTAL N_____ | TOTAL S_____ |

## Dimension

| T | F | P | J |
|---|---|---|---|
| **Item** | **Item** | **Item** | **Item** |
| 3a. _____ | 3b. _____ | 4a. _____ | 4b. _____ |
| 7a. _____ | 7b. _____ | 8a. _____ | 8b. _____ |
| 11a. _____ | 11b. _____ | 12a. _____ | 12b. _____ |
| 15b. _____ | 15a. _____ | 16a. _____ | 16b. _____ |
| 19b. _____ | 19a. _____ | 20b. _____ | 20a. _____ |
| 23b. _____ | 23a. _____ | 24b. _____ | 24a. _____ |
| 27a. _____ | 27b. _____ | 28a. _____ | 28b. _____ |
| 31b. _____ | 31a. _____ | 32b. _____ | 32a. _____ |
| TOTAL T_____ | TOTAL F_____ | TOTAL P_____ | TOTAL J_____ |

## Perceiving—Judging

The perceiver is a gatherer, always wanting to know more before deciding, holding off decisions and judgments. As a consequence, the perceiver is open, flexible, adaptive, non-judgmental, able to see and appreciate all sides of issues, always welcoming new perspectives and new information about issues. However, perceivers are also difficult to pin down and may be indecisive and non-committal, becoming involved in so many tasks that do not reach closure that they may become frustrated at times. Even when they finish tasks, perceivers will tend to look back at them and wonder whether they are satisfactory or could have been done another way. The perceiver wishes to roll with life rather than change it.

The judger is decisive, firm, and sure, setting goals and sticking to them. The judger wants to close books, make decisions, and get on to the next project. When a project does not yet have closure, judgers will leave it behind and go on to new tasks and not look back.

## B. COMMUNICATION SKILLS: SELF-DISCLOSURE

In every process of communication, we are both senders and receivers of messages, verbally and non-verbally, by act and by omission. It is impossible not to communicate. Think of the powerful message that may be read in the phone call not returned or the letter not answered. But it is often appallingly difficult to communicate exactly what we intended to say. The next sections proceed from (1) the johari window as a useful model for conceptualizing the communication process, to (2) the skills of self-disclosure necessary for the sender, then (3) the listening skills necessary for the receiver, and finally (4) the skills of giving and receiving feedback necessary to sustain the communication at a more than superficial level.

## 20. THE JOHARI WINDOW

The johari window (named for its originators, psychologists Joseph Luft and Harry Ingham) offers a convenient way for understanding the skills involved in interpersonal communication.

|  | Known to self | Not known to self |
|---|---|---|
| Known to others | I<br>Public area | II<br>Blind spot |
| Not known to others | III<br>Hidden area | IV<br>Unknown area |

I. *The Public Area* contains the data known both to the self and to others, e.g., that I have brown hair, that I am male or female, that I speak English.

II. *The Blind Spot* contains data known to the others but not to the self, e.g., how the back of my head looks, that there is a spot on the seat of my pants, some facial mannerism of which I am unaware.

III. *The Hidden Area* contains certain things known to the self but not to the others either because there has been no opportunity to reveal them or because I really wish to keep them hidden: e.g., where I was born, my mother's maiden name; or, in the second category, my age, that I have three false teeth, how much I earn.

IV. *The Unknown Area* is the wellspring of energy, creativity, and surprise, for it holds all the potentialities that are known neither to the self nor to the other. This material is below the level of conscious awareness, but some elements of it may emerge in a free, open and supportive interchange.

The larger the public area, the easier it is for a group to work together, since more of the skills and resources of the group members are available for the task at hand. The larger the public area in a relationship between two people, the greater the possibility for closeness and intimacy.

The public area can be enlarged by *self-disclosure,* that is, when a person begins to share his or her perceptions, feelings and thoughts openly with another or with a group. Two sets of skills are necessary for successful self-disclosure: (1) the skills of *expression,* of sending clear messages on the part of the discloser; and (2) the skills of *listening,* of receiving messages sensitively and accurately on the part of the other.

The other way to enlarge the public area is through feedback, that is, through the other revealing to the self some of the contents of the blind spot, specifically, how the self is perceived by the other. Feedback allows us "to see ourselves as others see us"; it can tell us what effect our behavior is having on them. Again, two sets of skills are necessary: those for giving and those for receiving feedback.

Any change in one area will affect all the others. It takes energy to hide or to be blind to behavior which is involved in an interaction. Therefore, self-disclosure and feedback tend to release energy and to enhance freedom of action. In a group with a high degree of mutual trust and openness, the release of energies may tap into the unknown area, producing flashes of insight and creativity previously unsuspected either by the self or the others.

*Objective:*

**To enable participants to practice using the johari window.**

a. Divide into trios.
b. Each person draws a johari window for himself or herself and writes down two items in the public area.

c. Each person then writes down in window III something from his or her hidden area. Each person is free to choose what he or she wishes to reveal about himself or herself and should do only what he or she is comfortable with.

d. Feedback: each person tells the other two something he or she may not know about himself or herself. He or she can write it in his or her blind window. Remember that all are free to choose what they want to say and how much risk they feel comfortable in taking.

e. Discuss in total group:

- What happened in your trio? any insights? surprises?
- How comfortable/uncomfortable were you in self-disclosure? in giving feedback?

*Note:* An additional step in a group whose members know each other fairly well: Each member draws a johari window for the other two in the trio, filling in the windows with data observed during the group interaction. Persons exchange drawings, discuss differences in perceptions, feelings.

## 21. GETTING STARTED

*Objectives:*

**To practice self-disclosure in a non-threatening way.**

**To "break the ice" in an initial group meeting.**

*Materials:*

"Getting Started" Sheets. (Cf. Work Sheet Ex. 21)

a. Pass out "Getting Started" sheets and give participants five minutes to reflect and fill them out.

b. Participants mill and pair; communicate, using their sheets as a starting point.

c. Each participant introduces partner. Partner may correct or add to introduction.

d. Discuss:

- How did you feel during the exchange with partner?
- How would you compare this introduction to a first conversation in a conventional social setting?

## 22. DRAWING YOURSELF

*Objectives:*

**To practice self-disclosure**

**To increase awareness of non-verbals**

*Resources:*

Trained facilitator.

Large sheets of newsprint or brown paper for each participant; crayons or magic markers in a variety of colors.

a. Each participant is asked to draw important aspects of his or her present life that he or she wishes to share with this group. Skill in drawing is not important; the object is for all to represent, in any way they can, using colors on paper, aspects or elements of their life at present. Allow ten to fifteen minutes for the drawing.

b. Form small groups of three or four people. Each person shares a drawing. The others "read" the picture. Remember to distinguish between "I see" and "I think" statements.

- What do you actually see in this picture?
- What conclusions are you drawing from your observations?

The owner then explains. Participants should be aware that this exercise often has elements of surprise for the maker of the drawing, who may need support at the moment of unsettling insight. Relative size and placement of elements, choice of colors, strength or weakness of lines, whether the person uses the whole sheet or only a part, may reveal new aspects of the self.

It is important to realize that the maker of the drawing is the ultimate authority on his or her feelings and intentions and that the maker has the right to reject the others' interpretations of the work.

c. Discuss in total group:

- Did you discover anything new about yourself from the drawing? from the comments?
- How does this form of getting acquainted compare with other forms you have experienced?

*Note:* Alternative exercise:

- Draw your lifeline, from birth to death, marking the present moment, the high and low points, etc.

## 23. DESCRIBING YOU, DESCRIBING ME

*Objectives:*

**To encourage free association about self and another.**

**To use such free association as a means of increasing self-awareness.**

**To use such free association as a means of building trust between partners.**

a. Group members are asked to stand up and move around the room in silence. After a few moments, they are asked to choose someone they would like to get to know better. No one should assist participants in making this choice.

b. Pairs find comfortable seating, then are asked to spend two or three minutes writing a "free associ-

## *Getting Started*

This sheet is meant as a thought starter. Find a place in the room where you feel comfortable, reflect a bit, and then complete the following sentences with as many words or phrases as come to mind.

1. Something that I liked that happened to me in the last twenty-four hours was

2. Something I disliked that happened to me in the last twenty-four hours was

3. I get very enthusiastic about

4. I get upset by

5. The thing I would most like to change in this world is

6. Something I particularly like to do is

7. Something important to me that I want to share in this group is

8. Something I am hoping for from this group is

ation" description of themselves. (See Ex. 10, AUTOMATIC WRITING, earlier for detailed instructions.)

c. Participants are asked to repeat the free association process, this time writing a description of the partner.

d. Partners share their writings and discuss:

- Were there similarities and differences between self-description and description by partner?
- Did any parts of your partner's description of you sound familiar? Did any of it seem inaccurate?
- How do you feel at the end of this exercise? Do you notice any difference as compared to when you began?

e. Allow time for sharing of insights and comments in the total group.

## 24. SHARING SECRETS

*Objective:*

**To enable participants to experience self-disclosure as freeing.**

a. To preserve anonymity, provide identical pencils and cards or slips of paper for everyone.

b. Each person jots down on the card a secret about himself or herself that has never been shared with anyone.

c. The cards are folded and placed in a container. Each person draws one and reads it aloud.

d. The group discusses each secret as read, without breaching the anonymity. There is a freeing aspect simply in being able to share a secret anonymously. Moreover, quite often the person discovers that something he or she has been hiding as a "dark secret" is not regarded as "dark" by others, or is something which others in the group have also experienced.

At the end of the exercise, the cards are gathered up and destroyed.

## 25. DISCLOSING NEGATIVE FEELINGS*

Many of us are able to express warmth, caring and love, but have a difficult time sharing so-called negative feelings like anger. Sometimes we may have difficulty even admitting these to ourselves. This exercise is intended to show that venting such feelings is not necessarily bad, and may actually have a freeing and healing effect. These exercises should only be attempted

---
*This exercise contributed by Mark Young, Ohio University.

when the participant is entirely willing. They should never be attempted by an inexperienced group leader, since the release of strong negative feelings often leads to deeper emotional expression of rage, abandonment or sadness, and can induce a lengthy period of weeping. The group needs to be highly cohesive and caring, with enough time to provide support and closure for the individual who has been the focus of the exercise.

These exercises are usually not planned ahead of time, but are utilized when a group member is unable to deal verbally with feelings.

*Objectives:*

**To enable participant to vent anger in a safe environment.**

**To demonstrate that venting of anger can be freeing.**

*Resources:*

A trained facilitator.

A large firm pillow or a batacca (pillow stick), or a pillow in an oversized pillow case so that the individual can grasp the ends and bang the pillow against a chair or the floor.

a. The participant kneels on the floor with the pillow in front of him or her and is asked to pound the pillow rhythmically with both fists. The facilitator remains close by for reassurance.

b. While pounding, he or she repeats an appropriate phrase, like "Leave me alone!" "No!" "Let me go!" "Get off my back!" "I hate you!" or some other phrase that occurs to the person.

c. An alternative exercise:

The participant is asked to role play the situation he or she is angry about, choosing another group member to represent the other party in the situation. They stand on opposite sides of a chair with a pillow placed on it. As the person begins to express his or her anger verbally, he or she is asked to use blows on the pillow to emphasize the statements as a kind of exclamation point.

d. Discuss in total group:

- How does the participant feel at the end of the exercise?
- How do other members of the group feel as they watch the open expression of anger? Were they aware of changes in breathing? muscular tension? butterflies in the stomach?
- Were you reminded of anything in your experience as you watched?
- How were you taught to deal with angry feelings?
- If anger is not expressed, what happens to it?
- Share your feelings and support with the participants in this exercise.

## 26. ACTING OUT ANGER BETWEEN GROUP MEMBERS*

Sometimes resentment builds up between group members. Often it is useful to discharge anger and/or hostility through action before attempting to resolve it verbally.

*Objectives:*

**To demonstrate a safe way of venting anger promptly rather than allowing it to build up.**

**To demonstrate that non-verbal release of feeling is an aid to resolving disagreements.**

Methods which can be used to allow individuals in conflict with each other to act out their feelings:

a. Indian wrestling: two persons face each other, hold right hands, elbows on table or floor. The object is to push against the other's hand until it touches the surface.

b. Mock battle with batacca bats or bats made of rolled up newspaper.

Verbal resolution can then be attempted. Discussion in total group can follow same line as in #25 above.

## C. COMMUNICATION SKILLS: ACTIVE LISTENING

Communication is a twofold process, depending for its success on sensitive receiving of messages as much as on clear sending. The skills of active listening are the skills of the receiver. It is not enough to be within earshot and let the message wash over one. Listening is an active process, demanding focused attention, awareness of non-verbals, careful checking of one's perceptions. This section provides an introduction to some of these skills.

## 27. MIRRORING

*Objectives:*

**To increase awareness of non-verbals.**
**To increase attentiveness to the other.**

a. Participants pair and stand facing each other.
b. Ask one participant to take the role of the sender of messages, and the other to become the mirror. The sender can do anything he or she wishes—pretend to be getting dressed, express feelings, make faces, whatever. The "mirror" attempts faithfully to reflect whatever the sender does.
c. Reverse roles.
d. Discuss, first in dyads, then in total group:

- How did you feel as sender? as mirror?
- Does the sender think he or she was reflected accurately by the mirror?

- Did you learn anything about your attentiveness in this exercise? about the other aspects of yourself?

## 28. MAKING CONTACT WITH OTHERS*

Communication is a process of reaching out in order to make contact with others. But often we are ambivalent about contact: we want closeness, we want to be understood and to understand, but we also want privacy and fear intrusion.

*Objective:*

**To enable participants to explore their feelings about contact and private space.**

a. Ask participants to arrange their chairs in a circle.
b. All close their eyes and in silence proceed to explore their space, stretching out hands and feet in all directions—up, down, left, right, forward, back—exploring their space as fully as possible, while still remaining seated.
c. After three or four minutes of exploring the space, all open their eyes and discuss:

- How close are you to the nearest member of the group?
- Did anyone leave his or her chair somewhat outside the circle? Does this spatial arrangement reflect anything about the relationship of person to group?
- How did you feel when exploring your space with your arms and legs?
- Did you touch anyone else during your explorations? Did anyone touch you?
- How did you feel about touching or being touched? Did you feel you were intruding? being intruded upon?
- Do you feel you have enough space? Do you feel others are crowding in on you? Do you feel others are too distant from you?
- What do you think about the relation of physical distance to the ability to make contact with others?

## 29. RECEIVING MESSAGES —A GET-ACQUAINTED EXERCISE

*Objective:*

**To increase attentiveness to the sender.**

a. Participants form circles of six to eight persons each.
b. Each person takes a turn, giving his or her name and favorite color, using an "ing" verb to describe

---

*This exercise contributed by Mark Young.

*Adapted from Andrew Panzarella, *Microcosm.* St. Mary's College Press, Winona, Minn., 1972.

some personal characteristic, and mentioning a current concern.

c. Participants then turn their chairs around, so that they have their backs to each other, and jot down what they remember.

d. They turn back to the circle and share what they have written.

e. Discuss:

- How much were you able to remember of what each person said?
- What helped?
- What hindered?

# 30. PERCEPTION CHECKING

*Objectives:*

**To increase awareness of differences between observations and inferences.**

**To practice checking inferences with the other.**

a. Participants are invited to choose a partner whom they do not know very well.

b. A describes B, drawing some inference from the observation, according to the following pattern:

  A. I see that you are tapping your left foot, and I think that indicates tension. I think you may be feeling nervous in this situation. Is that so?

  B. Responds.

c. Reverse roles and repeat.

d. Discuss:

- How did you feel when the other described you?
- What are some consequences of failing to check out perceptions?

e. Facilitator can stop the discussion at a given moment and ask each group member to jot down how he or she feels about the discussion at that moment, i.e., positive or negative.

Then each member jots down how he or she thinks each other is feeling. Each member's self-evaluation is put on the board. The group is then polled: "How many guessed that Jane was feeling positive?"

Individuals then interview those whose feelings they misread to discover the cause of the misreading.

Group discusses ways to improve accuracy, factors that prevent us from perceiving accurately.

This exercise can be repeated several times, using statements about which there is a difference of opinion in the group, so that members can improve their accuracy of perception.

# 31. LISTENING TRIOS

*Objectives:*

**To give practice in paraphrasing and empathizing.**

**To give practice in clear expression of thoughts and feelings.**

a. Form groups of three.

b. A shares with B around some topic, e.g.,

- some important things that have been happening in my life lately.
- what I like best about myself.
- something I am really concerned about right now.
- something I'd like to change about myself.

B tries to be a sympathetic listener—drawing A out, paraphrasing, reflecting A's feelings. C observes the conversation, paying attention to clear expression by A, accuracy of paraphrasing and identification of feeling by B.

c. After three to five minutes, C feeds back observations.

d. Continue exercise until each person has had a turn in all three roles.

e. Discuss:

- What difficulties did you experience in each role?
- What barriers do you observe to effective listening?
- How effective was your self-expression?
- Check your observations against the sheet on "Some Behaviors of a Good Listener." (Cf. Work Sheet Ex. 31.)

# 32. DEALING WITH "MIXED MESSAGES"

Sometimes the other sends a "mixed message"—that is, the gestures and body language or tone of voice seems contrary to the verbal content, or one part of the content seems to contradict the other part. Understandably, mixed messages are often confusing to the receiver, who needs the skill to disentangle the two messages and check perceptions with the sender.

*Objectives:*

**To practice disentangling mixed messages.**

**To practice perception checking on mixed messages.**

a. Choose a partner and sit facing each other. Begin a conversation, with A taking care to cancel his or her statements non-verbally—by a laugh, tone of voice, gesture, wink, or whatever.

b. Reverse roles, with B doing the non-verbal cancelling.

## *SOME BEHAVIORS OF A GOOD LISTENER*

1. Check the physical surroundings to eliminate distractions and interference: noise, heat or cold, distance, seating, symbolic barriers.
2. Be attentive—give your full attention, undivided, to the other.
3. Use supportive non-verbals; eye contact, smiles, nods and other gestures.
4. Use "door openers":

   - I see.
   - Hmm.
   - How about that.
   - Tell me more.
   - Would you like to talk about it?
   - This seems like something important to you.
   - I'd like to hear about it.
   - Interesting.
   - You don't say.
   - No fooling.
   - Shoot, I'm listening.

5. Paraphrase: check that you are hearing the content accurately. "I hear you saying. . . ."
6. Check your perceptions: "I think you're feeling. . . . Is that so?"
7. Accept the feelings of the other person as facts; don't tell the other that he or she cannot or does not or should not feel that way.
8. Avoid closed questions, i.e., questions which indicate which answer you expect: "You're not going, are you?"
9. Avoid "door closers," i.e., forms which tend to arouse defensiveness.

   - You have to go.
   - You'd better not try that.
   - You shouldn't feel that way.
   - Why don't you do what I do?
   - Here are the facts.
   - What you need is . . .
   - The trouble with you is . . .
   - Let's forget it.
   - You're wrong.
   - You're right.
   - You're stupid; you should know better.
   - Why did you?
   - You always . . .
   - You never . . .

10. Give honest feedback on mixed messages: "You are saying 'yes,' but you're frowning."

c. Share with your partner:

- How did it feel to be on the receiving end of a mixed message?
- What means did you use to cancel your messages?
- Did either of you use a verbal message where one part cancels the other, e.g., "I like you—you're such a cute little dope"?
- How did you attempt to deal with the mixed message?

d. Repeat the experience, but this time the receiver consciously tries to separate the two parts of the message and either (1) asks for clarification—"What are you telling me?" or (2) indicates clearly which part he or she is responding to—"I hear 'dope' wrapped up in that sweet message, and I don't like that."

## 33. IDENTIFYING THE OTHER'S FEELING*

*Objective:*

**To identify the other's feeling when it is not expressed directly.**

a. Participants use work sheet Ex. 33, "Recognizing Feelings," jotting down the feelings they identify behind the statements.
b. Pair and share results.
c. Discuss in total group.

## 34. ROLE REVERSAL

*Objective:*

**To give experience of entering into another's viewpoint.**

a. Group chooses an incident to role play, e.g.:

- student and teacher discussing a change of grade
- husband and wife planning a summer vacation
- daughter asking for family car for the evening
- customer returning defective merchandise to clerk

or any other situation that presents a problem in communication.

b. After five minutes of play, stop the action and reverse the roles.
c. Discuss:

- How did you feel in the first role? in the second role?
- Did your perceptions of the situation change when you changed roles?

---

*Adapted from Thomas Gordon, *P.E.T.: Parent Effectiveness Training.* New American Library, N.Y., 1975.

- Did your feelings change when you changed roles?

## 35. ALTER EGOS

*Objective:*

**To give practice in identifying thoughts and feelings of another.**

a. A small group—three to five people—sit in the inner circle and engage in some task: they may role play a situation or engage in a problem solving exercise. Cf. Pfeifer and Jones, *Handbooks of Structured Experiences for Human Relations Training,* for possible tasks.
b. One person is assigned to be the alter ego of each individual in the inner circle, and sits or stands directly behind his or her member.
c. From time to time, as the discussion proceeds, the alter ego states what he or she thinks his or her member is feeling or thinking, indicating the desire to speak by placing a hand on the other's shoulder. The alter ego then checks the perception with the person involved.
d. After ten or fifteen minutes, reverse roles, with the alter egos in the inner circle, and a new task for the group.
e. Discuss:

- What clues did the alter egos use in making their comments?
- What effect do the interventions have on the group task?

## 36. COMMUNICATING WITH DIFFERENT PERSONALITY TYPES

Persons of the same personality type tend to gravitate together, communicate easily and reach decisions easily, while those who differ strongly on the various Jungian dimensions may have difficulty in understanding each other and working together. However, if persons of opposite type can learn to communicate with each other, their interaction will benefit from the strengths of each type.

*Objective:*

**To develop skill in communicating with persons of a personality type different from one's own.**

a. Use the Personality Style Inventory (cf. Ex. 19) to determine personality types. Note that what Blaker in Chapter 10 of *Readings in Value Development* calls "analytic" the Inventory calls "thinking," and that Blaker's contrast between "flow" and "structure" is called "perceiving" vs. "judging" in the Inventory.

# WORK SHEET EX. 33

## *Recognizing Feelings*

Read each item separately, trying to listen carefully for feelings. Then in the right hand column write the feeling or feelings you perceive. Discard the content and write in only the feeling—usually one or several words. Some statements may contain several different feelings; write all the main feelings you perceive.

*The other person says:*                                        *The other is feeling:*

1. I don't know what's wrong—I'm just not getting anywhere. Maybe I should just quit trying.

2. For all the attention anyone pays me in this place, I might as well not be here.

3. If things don't improve around here, I'll look for a new job.

4. That teacher is awful. She didn't teach me a thing.

5. Can't you see I'm busy?

6. The deadline for this term paper is just not realistic.

7. I'd sure like to go, but I just can't call her up. What if she'd laugh at me?

8. I'm putting in a lot of time practicing, but I don't get the results Anne does.

9. Why did old Mr. Sawyer make me stay after class? I wasn't the only one who was talking.

10. I'd like to go on to college, but I don't know if I can make the grade.

Each person could wear a card with his or her code on it, e.g., ENTJ, ISFP, INTP, etc.

b. Form groups of three with the maximum amount of difference in type.

c. A and B attempt to dialogue with each other about a task they are to accomplish. C monitors the dialogue, noting particularly the efforts to paraphrase, to use the other's language, and to check perceptions.

d. Repeat, until each member of the trio has had a turn in all three roles.

e. Discuss:

- What difficulties did you experience in trying to speak the language of your opposite number?
- What do you see as the advantages of your opposite's type?
- What do you see as the advantages of your own type?
- What do you see as the disadvantages of your own type? of the other's type?
- Can you draw any practical implications for your own behavior from this exercise?

# D. COMMUNICATION SKILLS:  GIVING AND RECEIVING FEEDBACK

The notion of "feedback" comes from the field of automation. Feedback is any information about the result of a process, especially when used as an input to maintain the output within certain limits. Thus, the thermostat gives feedback to the furnace on how well it is heating the house, and this information either turns the furnace on or turns it off automatically.

In the process of interpersonal communication, feedback means giving the other information on how his or her behavior is affecting you. To return to the johari window, feedback is information coming from Area II, the blind spot. However, unlike the automation process, the communication process requires choices both on the part of the giver and the receiver of feedback. The following "Notes on Feedback" indicate the main elements to be considered.

Feedback is the communication to another person of information about how his or her behavior is affecting you. It is not a demand for change, but rather the giving of some relevant information. It leaves the receiver free to decide what use, if any, he or she will make of the information. Feedback helps a person to learn from experience; it enables him or her to check on how well his or her behavior matches his or her intentions; it increases his or her options. The following guidelines indicate more and less effective ways of giving feedback.

## ON THE PART OF THE GIVER OF FEEDBACK

Feedback is *more effective* when it is:

1. *Asked for* or there are other clear indications that the receiver is ready for it.
2. *Descriptive:* A clear report of the facts rather than your ideas about why things happened or what they mean. Stick to "I see," "I hear," I feel." Use direct quotes and examples.
3. *Specific:* "When you interrupted Helen just now, I felt annoyed."
4. *About modifiable behavior.*


5. *About observable behavior.*
6. *Recent:* Usually, it is most useful when given at the earliest opportunity after the behavior.
7. *Given at an appropriate time:* It should be given when there is a good chance it can be used.
8. *Given to be helpful:* Giver needs to consider his or her own motives.

9. *Not Demanding a change,* but trying to make new data available to the receiver.
10. *One point at a time.*

Feedback is *less effective* when it is:

1. *Imposed:* If not ready, the receiver will be apt not to hear it or to misinterpret it.
2. *Evaluative:* "You're pushy/dominating/lazy/selfish," or whatever other label.


3. *General:* "You always try to boss the show/You never do your share."
4. *About behavior not under the control of the receiver,* e.g., a nervous tic, an habitual mannerism, a physical characteristic.
5. *About motives or intentions.*
6. *Ancient history:* "When you called me last month. . . ."
7. *At an inappropriate time:* e.g., if the receiver is very busy, preoccupied, depressed.
8. *For the giver:* To enable the giver to relieve anxieties, demonstrate superiority, control the other, etc.
9. *Demanding a change:* "I've told you what's wrong with you; now it's up to you to change!"
10. *An overload.*

## ON THE PART OF THE RECEIVER OF FEEDBACK

1. Remember you are free to decide what use, if any, you will make of the information.

2. Remember that feedback helps you to learn from experience. It enables you to check on how you are coming across to the other, how clearly you are expressing your feelings, how well your behavior matches your intentions.

3. It is helpful to ask for feedback, and to mention specific points on which you would like feedback.

4. It is helpful to check whether you have heard accurately by paraphrasing what has been said.

5. It is helpful to thank or otherwise reward the giver of feedback, if you wish the feedback to continue. The giver of feedback has probably taken a risk in offering the comment, and may be anxious about it, so it is important to show your appreciation, along with whatever other feelings you may be having.

6. Share your feelings, but try not to get defensive or get into an argument about the content. Remember that all you need to do is to take this bit of information under consideration.

## 37. THE GIFT OF HAPPINESS: GIVING AND RECEIVING POSITIVE FEEDBACK

*Objective:*

**To practice giving and receiving positive messages.**

a. Each participant takes off one shoe and puts it in front of him or her to serve as a mailbox.

b. Group has twenty minutes in which to write messages:

- addressing each message to a specific person, by name.
- writing in the first person, "I see . . . I like . . ."
- being honest, clear and precise about something positive you have observed in the other, why you are glad to be in the group with him or her, etc.
- signing or not as you choose.

c. Messages are delivered. Each person reads his or her own.

d. Discuss:

- What feelings come up when you are acknowledge positively?
- Was it difficult for anyone to receive positive feedback? Did you find yourself spontaneously thinking, "Yes, but . . ."?
- In trying to be specific in your positive message, did you become aware of something you had not noticed before?

- Did you find it easier to give or receive positive feedback?
- Are any of the messages ambiguous? If the message is signed, ask the sender to clarify.

## 38. SYMBOLIC FEEDBACK

*Objective:*

**To develop skill in expressing feedback symbolically.**

a. Each person takes a turn at becoming the focus of the group.

b. Other members of the group think of an animal which they associate with the receiver of the feedback. "If you were an animal, I think you would be a. . . ."

c. Discuss:

- How do you feel about your animal "portraits"?
- What reasons did the giver of the feedback have for the choice?

d. Alternatives: a plant, a tree, a kind of automobile, a flower.

## 39. A FEEDBACK EXPERIMENT

*Objectives:*

**To develop ease in requesting feedback.**
**To develop skills in giving feedback.**

*Resources:*
A trained facilitator.

a. Facilitator calls for three volunteers. Each volunteer asks the group for feedback on the impression he or she is making on the group.

b. Facilitator asks the group to think of ways in which any two of the three are like each other and different from the third. Members take a few minutes to write down as many points as they can in all possible combinations of three people taken two at a time.

c. Members take turns giving their perceptions of the similarities and differences.

d. The three receivers of feedback then respond:

- asking for clarifications, if any are needed.
- sharing their feelings.

e. Facilitator asks for three other volunteers, and continues with the exercise until all who wish have had the opportunity to volunteer.

## 40. A FIRST EXPERIENCE WITH FEEDBACK

*Objectives:*

**To give experience in asking for feedback.**

**To practice skill of giving specific, non-evaluative feedback.**

a. Each group member writes a question concerning something he or she wants to know about himself or herself in the group.

b. Group members who so desire offer their comments, supporting their responses with specific examples.

c. Discuss:

- How do you feel in asking for feedback—comfortable? anxious? embarrassed?
- How do you feel in giving feedback?
- Did several persons note the same behavior?
- Did you make any discoveries about yourself? about the others?

# 41. RELATIONSHIPS: A FEEDBACK WORKSHEET*

*Objectives:*

**To practice giving feedback in a low risk situation, i.e., with the giver remaining anonymous.**

**To make explicit possibilities for relationships that may not have had opportunity to emerge in the group.**

*Resources:*

A trained facilitator.
Copies of Work Sheet Ex. 41.

a. Each member fills out the exercise sheet.
b. Facilitator collects the exercise sheets and collates the data on newsprint as follows:

|        | Jane | Jack | Harold | Mary | etc. |
|--------|------|------|--------|------|------|
| # (1)  | X    |      | X      |      |      |
| # (2)  |      | X    | X      |      |      |
| # (3)  | X    |      |        |      |      |
| etc.   |      |      |        |      |      |

c. Discuss:

- Did you want to put more than one person in some of the blanks?
- Had you previously expressed any of these feelings to the person concerned?
- Do you often find it difficult to express your positive feelings toward others?
- Were you aware of the relationships expressed toward yourself?
- How do you feel about others expressing their feelings toward you?

*Adapted from Andrew Panzarella, *Microcosm*. St. Mary's College Press, Winona, Minn., 1972.

- Was there anyone whose name did not appear on any of the sheets? What does this say about their participation in the group?

# 42. GROUP SCULPTURE

*Objectives:*

**To develop skill in expressing feelings toward another non-verbally.**

**To enable a group member to give non-verbal feedback to the group.**

a. One person volunteers to act as "sculptor." Others of the group are to act as "clay." One or two members are detailed to be "cameras," noting gestures and postures.

b. The sculptor then puts each group member in position, according to his or her perceptions of their closeness or distance from each other, their role in the group, their characteristic gestures and posture.

c. Discuss:

- The "cameras" feedback their observations.
- Group members share their feelings and perceptions, first of their own position, then of others in the sculpture.
- Observers and "sculptures" check their perceptions with the sculptor.

The experience may be repeated with another volunteer as sculptor. Variation: The sculptor may give each statue one line to speak either to the group or to an individual member.

# 43. SEEING OURSELVES AS OTHERS SEE US

> Oh, wad some power the giftie gie us
> To see ourselves as ithers see us . . .

The videotape machine and the tape recorder have quite literally answered Robert Burns' prayer. Most of us experience a shock the first time we receive feedback from these machines, so accustomed are we to viewing our behavior from the inside out, rather than to perceive ourselves from the outside. Either machine can be used in the following exercise.

*Objective:*

**To experience feedback from audio and/or videotape.**

a. Two or three people can either role play a situation or engage in a discussion of some topic that is personally involving, e.g., I am happiest when . . . The thing that turns me off most is . . . Something I do well . . . Something I'd like to change about myself . . .

## WORK SHEET EX. 41

Fill in the blanks with the names of members of your group.

1. The person in this group I would really like to get to know better is————————.

2. The person who seems most like myself is————————.

3. The person I would miss most if he or she were not here is————————.

4. The person who seems to understand me best is————————.

5. The person I understand best is————————.

6. The person I feel as most supportive of me is————————.

7. The person whose judgment I respect most is————————.

8. The person I perceive as most willing to take risks is————————.

**OBSERVER'S WORK SHEET EX. 43**

## I. Non-Verbal Behavior

| LISTENER/RESPONDER | SPEAKER |
|---|---|
| eye contact | |
| physical distance | |
| body direction (toward or away from the other) | |
| body gestures (withdrawn. . . . aggressive) (neutral. . . . supportive) | |
| body movement (rigid. . . . fluid) | |

## II. Verbal Behavior

| | |
|---|---|
| Door Openers (I see—tell me more—) | Speaks for self? for others? (I feel, I think, or we feel?) |
| Paraphrases content (I hear you saying . . .) | States points clearly |
| Checks own perceptions (I think you feel . . . ) | Gives examples |
| Describes behavior of others (descriptive, not evaluative language) | |
| Shares own feelings | |

Directions: Choose one person whom you are going to observe during the interaction. The sheet provides two columns, one for the speaker, the other for the listener/responder. In the top half of each column, record the non-verbal behaviors of your person as he or she speaks and listens, using check marks and/or short phrases. In the bottom half of each column, record verbal behaviors.

b. Continue the interaction long enough so that the participants have ceased to be aware of the recording device.

c. Other group members act as observers, using Work Sheet Ex. 43.

d. Replay the episode. The participants make notes on their own behavior; the observers add to their work sheets.

e. Discuss:

- How did the participants feel on seeing and/or hearing themselves? Any surprises?
- What did the participants notice about their own communication styles?
- What did observers notice? Did observers pick up additional points from the recording?

You may want to replay portions of the tape for close analysis. You may also wish to re-enact part or all of the original situation, with participants trying alternative behaviors.

## E. CARING AND INTIMACY

Caring implies a concern for the needs of others, which may range from simple solidarity to active cooperation, friendship, and deep intimacy. Caring requires an awareness of others' needs, a willingness to help meet them, and—if the relationship is one of a healthy interdependence—some skill in negotiating needs between the self and the other.

Hall defines intimacy as "a relationship in which I share my innermost being, my hopes and fears, anxieties and aspirations, my thoughts and emotions with another human being in such a way that I encourage him or her to feel free to do likewise." If caring is to develop into intimacy, it requires time, openness, commitment of both partners to sustained accountability, and skills in dealing with conflict. Intimates accept that their relationship is never static; they are flexible and never stop learning new ways to respond realistically to each other in the here and now.

## 44. AN EXERCISE IN GROUP PROBLEM-SOLVING*

*Objectives:*

**To check one's awareness of others' needs in a group situation.**

**To check one's willingness for collaboration.**

*Resources:*

A set of puzzles for each group of five participants. (Cf. Work Sheet 44c.)

---

*Adapted from Alex Bavelas: "The 5 Squares Problem: An Instructional Aid in Group Cooperation," in *Journal of the Acoustics Society of America,* 1950.

A set of instructions and rules for each group. (Cf. Work Sheet 44a.)

A guide sheet for each observer. (Cf. Work Sheet 44b.)

A facilitator to prepare the puzzles and lead the exercise.

a. The participants divide into groups of five plus an observer and seat themselves around a table.

b. The facilitator passes out one set of instructions to each group, reads the instructions, and answers questions for clarification.

c. Each observer is given an observer's guide sheet and is asked to make sure that the rules are strictly enforced.

d. At a signal from the facilitator, the groups open their envelopes and begin work. When all the groups have finished—or when most of the groups have finished and are anxious to move on—the facilitator calls time and opens the discussion, using some of the following questions:

- How did you feel during this problem-solving task?
- As you worked at the task, where did you tend to focus your attention?
- Who was willing to give away pieces?
- Who spotted another's need and supplied the necessary piece?
- Did anyone finish a square and then sit back?
- Did anyone break up a finished square for the sake of the group task?

Ask observer to feedback observations:

## 45. MUTUAL FUNDS

*Objectives:*

**To allow group members to appreciate the contributions of other participants.**

**To strengthen the cohesiveness of the group by bringing out similarities between people.**

*Materials:*

Play money in three or four denominations, the higher the better, in sufficient quantity so that every participant has one of each denomination.

a. Each person is asked to share with the group his or her (1) greatest fear, (2) greatest joy and (3) greatest hope. When everyone has had a turn, group members, one at a time, pass out their "funds" to the others based on their ability to relate to the hopes, fears, or joys of that individual. Funds may be disbursed to many people or in lump sums to one or two.

b. *Variation:*

This exercise can also be done at the end of a group meeting. Money is then paid out for *anything* some-

## *Instructions for Puzzle-Solving Group*

In the large envelope on your table are five smaller envelopes, one for each member of your group. When the signal is given, each member is to open his or her envelope and put the pieces of cardboard in front of them. The task of the group is to form five shapes of equal size. When the task is completed successfully, each member will have before him or her a geometric figure of the same shape and size as that held by each other member.

---

The following ground rules are to be observed:

1. No member may speak.
2. No member may ask another member for a piece or in any way signal that another is to give a piece to a specific person.
3. Members may give pieces to other members.
4. When a group has completed its task, the members are free to move around the room and observe other groups.

# WORK SHEET EX. 44B

## *Instructions for Observers*

Part of your job is to see that the rules are strictly enforced.

1. No talking, pointing, gesturing or any other kind of verbal or non-verbal communication among the five people.

2. Participants are allowed to give pieces to other participants, but may not take pieces from the others.

3. Participants must give their pieces to specific persons; they may not simply throw them in the middle for others to take.

4. Participants are free to give away all their pieces, even if they have already formed a finished square.

You may want to watch for the following behaviors:

1. Who is willing to give away pieces?

2. Does anyone finish quickly and then divorce himself or herself from the rest of the group?

3. Is there anyone who struggles with the pieces but is unwilling to give any of them away?

4. Who appears to notice what some of the others need?

5. Is anyone willing to break up a finished square?

6. How would you characterize the group climate? attentive and committed to the task? friendly or hostile? frustrated?

7. Did anyone simply give away all pieces and sit back, refusing to become involved?

8. Did anyone show impatience or irritation with a person who was slow at seeing the solution?

9. Did anyone spot another's need and supply the necessary piece?

10. How well did the group keep to the rules?

## *Directions for Making a Set of Set of Squares*

To prepare a set, cut out five cardboard squares of equal size, approximately 6 × 6 inches. Place the squares in a row and mark them as below, penciling the letters a, b, c, etc., lightly so they can later be erased.

The lines should be so drawn that, when cut out, all pieces marked "a" will be of exactly the same size, all pieces marked "c" of the same size, etc. By using multiples of three inches, several combinations will be possible that will enable participants to form one or two squares, but only one combination is possible that will form five squares six-by-six inches.

After drawing the lines on the six-by-six inch squares and labeling them with lower case letters, cut each

square as marked into smaller pieces to make the parts of the puzzle.

Mark the envelopes A, B, C, D, and E. Distribute the cardboard pieces in the five envelopes as follows:

Envelope A has pieces i, h, e.
Envelope B has pieces a, a, a, c.
Envelope C has pieces a, j.
Envelope D has pieces d, f.
Envelope E has pieces g, b, f, c.

Erase the penciled letter from each piece and write, instead, the appropriate envelope letter. This will make it easy to return the pieces to the proper envelope for subsequent use when a group has completed the task.

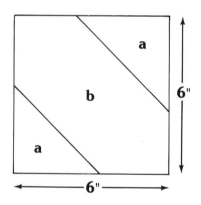

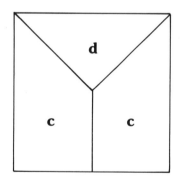

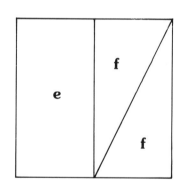

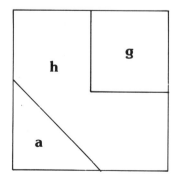

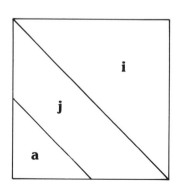

one might have said that was particularly meaningful, personally helpful or "close to home." As before, be sure that each participant specifies the reason for his or her payment.

c. Discuss:

- How did you feel as a receiver of funds? as a giver?
- Did you notice a variety of responses to receiving money?
- Did you notice the differing styles people used to pass out their funds?
- Was there anyone in the group who did not receive any funds? How do you feel about that? Can the group resolve this before it adjourns?
- When someone shares his or her vulnerability, how do you feel about him or her?

## 46. CONDITIONS FOR DEVELOPING A RELATIONSHIP TO THE LEVEL OF INTIMACY

*Objective:*

**To enable participants to clarify the meanings they attach to the notion of intimacy.**

a. Read Thomas Oden's conditions for intimacy on page 22 of "Skills for Growth" and restate them positively in your own words.

b. Discuss:

- Have you experienced any of these conditions?
- Do you agree that they are necessary, or disagree?
- Can you state the reasons for your agreement or disagreement?

## 47. EXPLORING VARIOUS DEFINITIONS OF INTIMACY

*Objectives:*

**To enable participants to analyze various definitions of intimacy.**

**To enable participants to identify elements they may wish to include in their own definition of intimacy.**

*Materials:*

The Gestalt Prayer of Fritz Perls. (Cf. *Gestalt Therapy Verbatim*. New York, Bantam Books, 1974.)
The Credo for Relationships by Thomas Gordon.
The Credo for Relationships by Virginia Satir. (Cf. Work Sheet Ex. 47.)

a. Read over these three statements by three well-known contemporary therapists who have had extensive experience in helping people improve their relationships.

b. Choose the two statements which most appeal to you. Try to identify the elements which each regards as important in an intimate relationship. What assumptions is each writer making about human beings, about change, about solitude, about commitment and accountability? What expectations would each have of "the significant other"?

c. Discuss with a partner or a small group.

d. Which elements, assumptions, expectations do you share?

## 48. DEVELOPING A PERSONAL CREDO

Each of us has his or her idea of a deeply satisfying human relationship. It is important to make explicit our assumptions and expectations and to test them against reality. Just as we can condemn ourselves to failure by holding ourselves to a standard of perfection, so we can destroy an otherwise fruitful relationship by making unrealistic demands on self and other.

*Objectives:*

**To enable participants to clarify their assumptions about intimacy and their expectations of self and other.**

**To enable participants to check the realism of their expectations.**

a. Write your own credo for relationships, taking account in some way of the following factors among others:
   —time
   —relationship to the future
   —openness to change in external circumstances, in self, in partner
   —accountability
   —control
   —conflict
   —commitment to one's personal growth
   —loneliness
   —solitude/privacy

b. Reread your credo and make a list of your assumptions, your expectations of yourself, your expectations of the other.

c. Share with a close friend. Discuss:
   —Are my assumptions well-founded?
   —Are my expectations realistic?

## 49. EXPRESSING WANTS AND NEEDS CLEARLY

This skill is particularly important for sustaining an intimate relationship, since we are all prone to assume, "If you really loved me, you would know what I want before I ask."

# WORK SHEET EX. 47

## *Two Credos for Relationship*

### Thomas Gordon's Credo for Relationships

You and I are in a relationship which I value and want to keep. Yet each of us is a separate person with his own unique needs and the right to try to meet these needs. I will try to be genuinely accepting of your behavior both when you are trying to meet your needs and when you are having problems meeting your needs.

When you share your problems, I will try to listen acceptingly and understandingly in a way that will facilitate your finding your own solutions rather than depending upon mine. When you have a problem because my behavior is interfering with your meeting your needs, I encourage you to tell me openly and honestly how you are feeling. At those times, I will listen and then try to modify my behavior.

However, when your behavior interferes with me meeting my own needs, thus causing me to feel unaccepting of you, I will tell you as openly and honestly as I can exactly how I am feeling, trusting that you respect my needs enough to listen and then try to modify your behavior.

At those times when neither of us can modify his behavior to meet the needs of the other, thus finding that we have a conflict-of-needs in our relationship, let us commit ourselves to resolve each such conflict without ever resorting to the use of either my power or yours to win at the expense of the other losing. I respect your needs but I also must respect my own. Consequently, let us strive always to search for solutions to our inevitable conflicts that will be acceptable to both of us. In this way, your needs will be met, but so will mine—no one will lose; both will win.

As a result, you can continue to develop as a person through meeting your needs, but so can I. Our relationship can always be a healthy one because it will be mutually satisfying. Thus, each of us can become what he is capable of being, and we can continue to relate to each other in mutual respect, friendship, love, and peace.

### Virginia Satir's Credo for Relationships

I want to love you without clutching
appreciate you without judging
join you without invading
invite you without demanding
leave you without guilt
criticize you without blaming
and help you without insulting.

If I can have the same from you
then we can truly meet
and enrich each other.

*Objective:*

**To express one's needs and wants clearly and specifically.**

a. Divide into groups of three to five people.

b. Each group member receives one slip, containing a vaguely worded need or want, e.g., "I want you to listen to me." One member asks the group to meet the need thus expressed. The others take turns making the need more specific, and hence achievable, by asking, "Do you mean you want me to put my book down?" "Do you mean you want me to tell you what I hear you saying?" etc. until they get at least three positive answers.

c. Discuss:
   —How did you feel when you first heard the request?
   —Do you make such requests in your daily life? or meet them from others?

d. Some sample statements that can be used in "b" above:
   —I want you to be more supportive.
   —I think the people in this group should trust each other more.
   —How can you be so sloppy?
   —It seems like a long time since we've had an evening together alone.
   —You should feel more self-confident.
   —I should be more organized.
   —I want you to love me.

## F. DEALING WITH CONFLICT

Conflict is an inevitable part of human life, a necessary condition for growth, and for the development of mutually rewarding relationships. However, to deal with conflict creatively and constructively requires skill. This section presents exercises and analysis toward that end.

## 50. BRAINSTORMING ASSOCIATIONS WITH "CONFLICT"

*Objective:*

**To enable group to get in touch with their dominant attitudes toward conflict.**

a. Group brainstorms associations with the word "conflict" as two recorders write down the words as fast as they come to mind.

b. Group goes through the list, evaluating the words as positive or negative. In most groups, the list will be overwhelmingly negative.

c. Discuss:
   —Why do we view conflict as negative?
   —What is the worst thing you can think of as happening as a result of conflict?
   —Can you see any advantages in conflict?

## 51. LECTURETTE ON CONFLICT

Conflict means to come into opposition, whether with weapons as in battle, or physically as in children's rough and tumble, or verbally as in a quarrel between friends.

*Objective:*

**To present an analysis of conflict.**

The outcomes of conflict as we know it are either:

a. Win/lose, which is the predominant form in our culture, where we tend to define situations—whether in sports, education, business or even personal relations—as competition for scarce resources: the trophy, the scholarship, the job.

b. Lose/lose. A win/lose approach leads easily into a lose/lose situation, since the anger and resentment of the loser does not disappear, but simply goes underground to emerge later as backlash. Thus in a quarrel between siblings, when the parent intervenes to establish Johnny's ownership of the toy, Tommy's resentment may express itself by breaking the toy so that neither one can play with it.

c. Win/win. Fortunately, we need not define every conflict situation as a competition for scarce goods. Because human beings are basically interdependent, the achievement of my goal may include the achievement of yours, as when the members of a consumer cooperative pool their efforts to improve the quality and reduce the costs of food to each member. Moreover, when we have identified a common goal, conflict, if openly surfaced and honestly faced, can improve both planning and implementation. More alternatives are likely to emerge from opposed views on how to proceed, and the resultant solution is apt to be better than that which any single participant could have produced.

Conflict is an inescapable part of human life. As soon as there are two people, there are two viewpoints and two sets of needs, which are bound to rub against each other some of the time. In any organized human effort, we must set up different roles and responsibilities, hence different needs and priorities. In a family, Dad needs a time of peace and quiet just when Johnny needs to blow off steam. In a business, the sales manager needs prompt delivery and hence wants a large inventory on hand, but the production manager wants a low inventory to keep down costs.

It would seem, then, that we do not have a choice about whether or not to encounter conflict; since conflict is inevitable, our only choice is how to deal with it. There are three basic ways of handling conflict:

1. Moving away from it either by total denial, or by suppressing or minimizing the differences, or by distracting ourselves and the other by changing the subject, or by giving in, surrendering, placating.

Partial or total suppression of conflict generally leads to physical and/or psychological sickness for the weaker party, or to manipulation and emotional blackmail which interferes with the relationship, and/or to an enlarged blindspot on the part of the more powerful party, and eventually an explosion of suppressed resentment in some form of aggression.

2. Moving against the other, fighting back in an attempt to overpower the other. This mode produces escalation in feelings of anger and hostility and in violence of actions and reactions.

3. Moving toward the conflict in an open confrontation. Confrontation is a way of using opposition constructively, trying to move from a win/lose toward a win/win situation. Confrontation requires a willingness to communicate, to explore alternatives and to increase options.

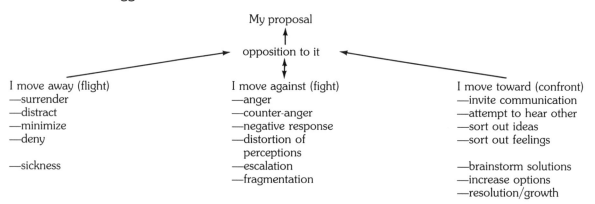

Another way to conceptualize the outcomes and strategies for dealing with conflict is illustrated by the diagram "Field of Conflict" where the two factors considered are concern for relationships (the right axis) and concern for tasks (the left axis).

## Field of Conflict

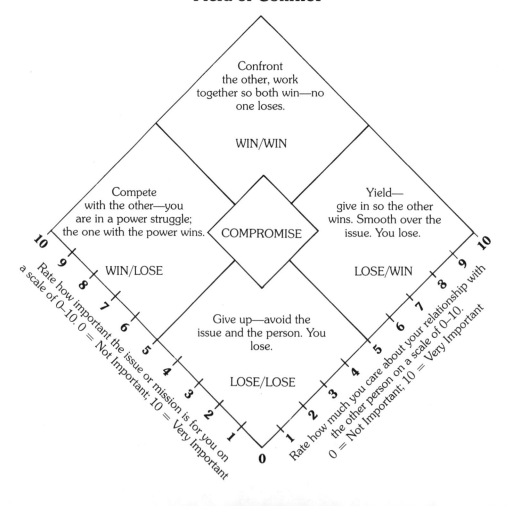

## 52. IDENTIFYING A CONFLICT SITUATION

*Objective:*

**To enable participants to identify a conflict situation in their own lives.**

**To enable each participant to identify the problem clearly.**

a. Fill out the scribble sheet (Ex. 52).
b. Pair and share with your partner.
c. Act as consultants to each other to enable each one to arrive at a clear definition of the problem. Ask:
   —What do I want in this situation?
   —Who owns the problem?

## 53. DECIDING WHETHER TO CONFRONT

*Objectives:*

**To enable participants to assess strengths and weaknesses of own position.**

**To enable participant to frame a strategy.**

a. Fill out scribble sheet (Ex. 53).
b. Pair and share with partner.
c. Act as consultant for your partner. Ask:
   —Are you willing to take the risk?
   —When do you plan the confrontation? Is the other in a state to listen?
   —Where do you plan it?
   —Are you confronting behavior or motives?
   —Can you be clear, concrete?
   —Have you looked at your own motives—are you fairly sure you are not meeting your own needs at the expense of the other?
   —How much are you willing to invest in working through the confrontation?

## 54. HOW TO CONFRONT*

The following formula puts in concise form all the elements for a successful confrontation:

—When you do A (describe specific action or words, in non-evaluative language)
—I feel B (name your feeling, without accusing the other, and without substituting your opinion for your feeling)
—and I want you to do C (be clear and specific about what you want from the other)
—because of D (appeal to a goal or value that you both share).

Be sure to state your positive intent; underline "D," that is, the common goal or value that you share with the other. Do not threaten or bribe.

*Adapted from Gracie Lyons, *Constructive Criticism*. Issues in Radical Therapy Press, Berkeley, Cal., 1973.

*Objective:*

**To enable participants to build skill in using the formula.**

a. Role play some of the following situations so that participants can gain facility in using the formula.
   —Worried parent confronting teenage daughter who stayed out till 3:00 A.M.
   —Employee confronting boss on the subject of a raise.
   —Wife confronting husband on the need to make vacation plans.
   —Worker confronting colleague who tries to get others to do his or her job.
b. Observers watch role plays and feed back observations.
   —Is language non-evaluative?
   —Do participants make clear statements of feelings?
   —Do participants make clear statements of intentions?
   —Do participants check perceptions and interpretations?

## 55. HOW TO HANDLE BEING CONFRONTED

*Objective:*

**To develop skill in responding non-defensively to attacks.**

a. Role play some of the following common attacks:
   —"You are always late!" (young woman to her date)
   —"You always hog the limelight!" (wife to husband on way home from party)
   —"Can't you ever get things straight? How many times must I tell you how I want this job done?" (employer to employee)
   —"It was not your place to make that suggestion." (one committee member to another after the meeting)
b. Some methods to use when someone confronts you:
   —Empathize with the other's feeling.
   —Paraphrase what the other is saying. ("I hear you saying. . . .") Be sure you have the message clear before you agree or disagree.
   —Ask questions to clarify what specifically you are doing that is the occasion for the other to call you "selfish," "arrogant," or whatever. Either ask for an example or ask "Do you mean . . . ?" questions.
   —Try to maintain a problem-solving attitude: you want to learn from the other's observations, feelings, wants.

A Scribble Sheet for Yourself: Ex. 52.

| | When I confronted someone | When I was confronted |
|---|---|---|
| 1. Who was involved? | | |
| 2. Relationship? | | |
| 3. Where? | | |
| 4. When? | | |
| 5. What did the other do? | | |
| 6. What did I do? | | |
| 7. How did I feel? | | |

## *Scribble Sheet: Deciding Whether to Confront*

1. What do I want in this situation?

2. Are my goals compatible with the goals of the other person?

3. Is this a survival situation for me, or is there a chance for a win/win resolution?

4. How much commitment to dialogue is there in this situation?

    —How willing am I to follow through on this confrontation?

    —How willing do I think the other person is?

5. What leverage do I have in this situation?

    —How much does the other value our relationship? my contribution to our common effort?

    —What allies do I have? (friends, fellow workers, a union, etc.)

6. How much risk am I willing to take?

# PART V:
# EXERCISES TO DEVELOP IMAGINAL SKILLS

All of us have imagination, the power that enables us to call up images out of our past experience, to rearrange and combine them in new ways, to see alternatives, to remedy deficiencies, to change conventional ways of doing things. But many of us either repress our imaginative powers for fear of ridicule and lack of confidence in our own perceptions, or we at least allow them to atrophy through disuse. We seldom set about deliberately to develop imaginal skills, and thus tend to remain passive, conforming to the environment rather than opening our eyes to new possibilities and taking initiative to bring them into being.

Moreover, much of formal education tends to direct our energies into what is called convergent thinking, that is, remembering and reproducing what is already known. We are trained to make the correct responses to pre-determined problems, and are rewarded for "right answers," i.e., those that conform to the guide in the back of the book. Of course, it is necessary to acquire skills in convergent thinking, but it is equally important to develop our capacity for its opposite, divergent thinking—the ability to create new wholes out of pre-existing elements, to explore the unstructured situation, to redefine the problem from a fresh angle, to generate the new, the unconventional, the original. Divergent thinking is open-ended in the sense that it invites in the unexpected and the unpredictable. Imaginal skills depend upon divergent thinking. Paul Torrance distinguishes four characteristics of divergent thinking:

1. *flexibility,* the ability to see with a fresh pair of eyes, to shift from one perspective to another, quite literally to move to a different standpoint;
2. *fluency,* an abundant flow of words, images, ideas;
3. *originality,* the capacity to produce fresh responses, arising out of each person's unique perspective, personal history and reactions;
4. *elaboration,* the ability to develop an idea or image, to make connections and fill in details.

However, before we can even begin to develop these various aspects of divergent thinking, we need to

break through the barriers imposed both by our internal censors and the censorship of the environment. It takes courage to be creative. Just as soon as the individual has a new idea, he or she becomes a minority of one, a position that most of us avoid almost by instinct. We have learned to be afraid of failing, of being different, of being laughed at, and if by chance a stray fantasy escapes our internal censorship, it is quickly put in its place by our friends, fellow students, co-workers or superiors. Therefore, this section begins with exercises intended "to break set," that is, to free up the imagination and to increase one's confidence in one's own perceptions, desires and dreams. When using this material in groups, particular care should be taken to set an open and supportive atmosphere, giving free rein to fantasy and "wild ideas," encouraging free associations, and withholding judgment and evaluation until the final stages of the process. We recommend reading pages 26-27 in Chapter 1, "Skills for Growth," which analyze behaviors that encourage or discourage creativity.

In each section, the exercises are arranged in a developmental sequence, moving from simpler to more complex tasks and from direct sensory experience to more abstract considerations of possibilities, values, courses of action, and social systems. The arrangement also proceeds from more structured to less structured starting points. In fact, some of the beginning exercises are instances of convergent rather than divergent thinking, e.g., the various puzzle exercises which admit of only one correct solution. These have been included to serve as a kind of intermediate step between the convergent and divergent modes, since their solution requires some breaking of set and/or flexibility and thus can help to build both skills and confidence. Initially, opening up too large a space for the imagination may prove bewildering or overwhelming. Thus, it is more difficult for most of us to respond to the directive to "write a story" than to respond to the directive to "write an ending to this story." The addition of boundaries or limiting conditions makes a project more tangible and imaginable. After individuals gain confidence in their own perceptions and fantasies, more open-ended projects can be used.

There is no section on originality as such. Each of us occupies a unique place in the universe, has a unique personal history, and therefore is capable of unique expressions. The problem is to enable people to discover their own uniqueness, and the various means suggested here contribute toward that end. Originality is a fruit of fluency, flexibility, freedom and self-confidence.

---

# Exercises To Free Up the Imagination

---

## 56. EXPERIENCING THE FORCE OF HABIT*
*Objective:*

**To become aware of the discomfort or resistance in ourselves to non-habitual behavior.**

a. Clasp your hands in front of you.
—Observe whether your right or your left thumb is on top.
—Tally responses in the group. Experiments have shown that groups tend to divide approximately in half in their habitual response.
—Now reclasp your hands, so that the other thumb is on top.
—Take a minute in silence to get in touch with how this feels: awkward? uncomfortable? strange? or equally comfortable either way?
—Share your findings.
b. Fold your arms in front of you. Repeat above steps.
c. Discuss:
—Can you identify other areas in your life where you have strong, almost automatic responses?
—What are the advantages and disadvantages of these responses?

## 57. THE NINE DOTS EXERCISE*
*Objective:*

**To experience "breaking set," i.e., identifying and discarding an unconscious assumption.**

a. Give each participant a copy of the following diagram.

b. The task is to connect all the dots by means of no more than four straight lines, without lifting the pencil from the paper and without passing through any dot more than once.
c. Allow five to ten minutes for participants to work on solutions.
d. Ask a participant to demonstrate the solution. (See page 134 for solution.)
e. Discuss:
—What procedure did you use in approaching the problem?
—What "set" did you adopt from the visual image?
—Did you become conscious of your "set"? Were you able to break out of it?
—Can you find examples of similar "sets" in your experience?

## 58. THE POVERTY GAME
*Objective:*

**To identify assumptions participants make about the rules and constraints in a situation.**
*Resources:*
Two trained facilitators

a. Divide the group into two parts, a small group of "haves" and a larger group of "have-nots." Announce that each group will have twenty minutes to consider its needs, desires and strategies before they meet together to negotiate.
b. One facilitator leads the "haves" to a comfortable meeting space, equipped with easy chairs, cushions, refreshments, etc., announces that their task is to decide how to deal with the "have-nots," and that he or she is now taking on the role of observer.
c. The other facilitator leads the "have-nots" to a small, crowded, uncomfortable space, e.g., a closet or a bathroom, announces that the task is to

---

*Adapted from Sidney J. Parnes, *Creative Behavior Guidebook.* Scribner's, New York, 1967.

discuss the needs of the "have-nots," and that he or she is now taking on the role of observer.

d. The observers note:
—How do individuals respond to their situation?
—Who takes the initiative to lead the "have-nots" out of their confinement?
—How long does it take for someone to take this initiative?
—Do the "haves" take any initiatives with respect to the "have-nots"?

e. Discuss:
—What assumptions is each group making about the limits of their situation? about what behavior is appropriate in their situation?
—There is a proverb to the effect that in Germany everything is forbidden except what is explicitly permitted, while in England everything is permitted which is not explicitly forbidden. Did the participants adopt the English or the German approach to the rules and regulations? What are the consequences of these two approaches?

## 59. REDEFINING THE PROBLEM

A problem is half-solved if it is properly stated. Often too narrow a statement of a problem may constitute a "set" that prevents a solution. To break out of the set, try to restate the problem as broadly as possible, so as not to preclude any answer. To arrive at a broader statement, it is helpful to ask "Why?" "What am I ultimately trying to accomplish?" Here are some common problems. See if by restating the problem in broader terms, you can come up with some possible solutions. (Solutions on page 134.)

*Objective:*
**To practice redefining problems in broader terms.**

a. A freight company based its charges on the weight of the merchandise. They were asked to ship barrels of chemicals that were so heavy it took four men to move them onto the scale. The manager did not have that much labor at his disposal and was puzzling over how to get the barrels onto the scale. Can you help him solve his problem?

b. The employee's work is unsatisfactory and the manager is wondering how to fire him with minimum repercussions. How would you do it?

c. Mary has been asked to chair the finance committee for her group, a very important and time-consuming task. She is deeply committed to the group and does not want to let them down, but

given her school work and part-time job, she does not have the time to do the committee work properly. She is torn between refusing the assignment and burning the midnight oil in order to fulfill it. What should she do?

d. John, a junior in college, is registered for a required course in his major which is given only in alternate years and meets Monday, Wednesday, and Friday at 10 A.M. He suffers from kidney disease and must spend every Monday morning at the hospital for a dialysis treatment, thus missing one-third of the class time. How can he rearrange his schedule?

## *Exercises for Developing Flexibility*

"Genius means little more than the faculty of perceiving in a unhabitual way."

Wm. James

## 60. SEEING SQUARES

*Objective:*
**To accustom the participants to view an object from different angles.**

a. How many squares do you see in the following diagram? Compare solutions. (Solution on p. 134.)

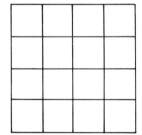

b. What shifts in viewpoint were necessary in order to see the various groupings?

c. Could you also see the drawing as a frontal view of a set of glass blocks, perfectly aligned and stretching on indefinitely into the distance?

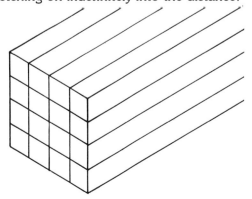

127

## 61. LOOKING AT 2 and 2
*Objective:*

**To view a familiar statement from fresh angles.**

a. How many ways can you interpret the question, "How much is 2 and 2?"
b. How did you approach this problem? Discuss. (Solution on page 134.)

## 62. MAKING PENTAMINOES*
*Objective:*

**To develop skill in seeing new relationships.**

a. A pentamino is a two-dimensional figure made up of five one-inch squares, each of which has at least one full side in common with at least one other square. A pentamino is different from other pentaminoes when it cannot be constructed by sliding, rotating or flipping any of the others.
b. Construct as many different pentaminoes as you can.
c. Discuss:
   —What methods did you use in making pentaminoes?
   —What helped you to discover new ones?
   —What hindered?

## 63. THE IMAGINARY BALL GAME
*Objectives:*

**To develop perception of non-verbal cues.**
**To develop ability to respond flexibly to changing cues.**

a. Players stand in a circle. One person initiates play with an imaginary ball. Players change the size and shape of the ball in the course of passing it to one another. Others respond appropriately.
b. Discuss:
   —How did you feel during the game?
   —Were you able to identify the kind of ball? to transform it?
   —How comfortable were you with sudden shifts in size and shape?

## 64. THE MAGIC BOX
*Objectives:*

**To develop non-verbal expression.**
**To develop perception of non-verbal cues.**

**To develop flexibility in responding to non-verbal cues.**

a. One person begins by miming the opening of an imaginary box, taking an object from it and passing it to someone in the circle. That person shows in mime that he or she grasps the identity of the object, then transforms it and passes it on.
b. Discuss:
   —How did you feel during the game?
   —Did transformations occur to you even when it was not your turn?
   —Were you able to read all the clues?

## 65. MAKING FRESH ASSOCIATIONS
"Everything is relevant; making things relevant is the creative process."

W. J. J. Gordon

From earliest childhood we have been taught to make certain associations between ideas or objects, e.g., bacon and eggs, dollars and cents, happy as a clam, bread and butter, clean as a whistle, drunk as a lord, and so on. Our speech and thoughts are full of such habitual, stereotyped patterns. One way to develop flexibility is to try consciously to relate unlike things.

*Objectives:*

**To develop fresh perceptions.**
**To develop ability to see the like in the unlike.**
**To develop the ability to generate similes and metaphors.**

a. Below is a list of unusual comparisons, which point up likenesses in things belonging to very different categories:
—Color likened to sound:

1. Black as a beating of drums.
2. Clouds as white as the bursting of a firecracker.

—Natural object likened to manufactured:

1. Clouds like flying ice cream.
2. Hair like spaghetti.
3. A poodle like a fluffy dust mop.

—Human to non-human:

1. Fingers like worms wriggling.
2. His anger was like a tornado.

—Small to large:

1. The needle is the locomotive and the thread is the train.

---

*Adapted from Leonard Davidman, "On Educating the Imagination: A Modest Proposal," in *Phi Delta Kappan,* Oct. 1980.

2. A top spinning like the rings of Saturn.

b. Think of some sense impression (a color, sound, shape, taste, smell, touch) and generate a list of comparisons. Let your imagination roam; try to find likeness across categories and between things that are usually considered to be totally unrelated.

c. Share with a partner or small group.

—Were you surprised by any of the comparisons?

—Did any of the comparisons seem forced?

—Did you find any methods that were helpful in generating new ideas?

---

# Exercises for Developing Fluency

---

"The way to have a good idea is to have lots of ideas."—Linus Pauling

## 66. OBSERVING A COMMON OBJECT
*Objectives:*

**To heighten sensory awareness.**
**To develop verbal fluency.**

a. Choose a common object—a ballpoint pen, a lead pencil, a penny, a leaf, a stone, your own hand. Each person should have the object at hand and be able to manipulate it.

b. For three to five minutes, examine the object and jot down as many words or phrases as possible to describe it in whole or in part.

c. Pair and share lists, paying special attention to the differences. Begin to develop categories from the differences, i.e., the way the object looks, feels, sounds, smells, tastes, its shape, parts, materials, functions, etc.

d. Repeat the exercise with a second object. Note whether fluency improves with practice.

## 67. DEVELOPING ALTERNATIVE BEHAVIORS
*Objective:*

**To imagine a variety of possible behaviors for oneself.**

a. Each person thinks of someone he or she is fond of and makes a list of ways to show positive feeling for this person.

b. Pair and compare lists.

c. Discuss:

—Did your partner think of alternatives that did not occur to you, and vice versa?

—How do you feel about actually trying some of the new possibilities?

## 68. "ONCE UPON A TELEPHONE POLE"
*Objective:*

**To illustrate the wealth of unsuspected possibilities that lie hidden in the most commonplace objects.**

a. Show the film, "Once Upon a Telephone Pole."

b. Discuss:

—What uses do the children find for the telephone poles?

—What has the artist Robert Wilson done that has enabled the children to see the poles in a new way?

—Can you think of other uses for old poles?

## 69. UNUSUAL USES OF A COMMON OBJECT*
*Objective:*

**To develop fluency and variety.**

a. Take a common object—cardboard box, tin can, pipe cleaner, wire coat hanger, ball of twine, broom, length of sewer pipe.

b. Examine the object; then jot down as many alternative uses for it as you can think of.

c. Compare lists, paying particular attention to unique responses.

## 70. PRODUCT IMPROVEMENT*
*Objective:*

**To develop fluency and flexibility.**

a. Choose a familiar product—e.g., a desk calendar, a woman's handbag, the family bathtub, a briefcase—and make suggestions for product improvement. What would make it more useful? more interesting? more fun to use?

b. Choose a children's toy—a small stuffed animal, a coloring book. What would make it more fun for children to play with? more stimulating to the child's imagination?

c. Compare lists.

## 71. SEEING CONSEQUENCES*
*Objective:*

**To develop the ability to play with an idea and to entertain possibilities.**

a. Suppose each person had a third eye, in the back of the head. What are some of the consequences that would result?

*Adapted from E. Paul Torrance, *Torrance Tests of Creative Thinking.* Personnel Press, Inc., Princeton, N.J., 1966.

b. Alternate suppositions:

- What if clouds had strings?
- What if human beings had no thumbs?
- What if the earth were covered with a dense fog, extending down to two feet above the ground?

c. Compare lists. Pay attention to unique and infrequent responses. Analyze shifts in perspective and categories involved in the responses.

## 72. EXPRESSING ALTERNATIVES THROUGH DRAWING*
*Objective:*
**To develop non-verbal fluency.**

a. Prepare a page of thirty geometric figures for each participant. Any figure can be used—circles, squares, parallel lines, ovals, triangles, pentagons—so long as they are all of the same size and are evenly spaced on the page.
b. The task is to make as many different objects as possible, incorporating the figure in each one.
c. Compare drawings. Note unique responses. Analyze shifts in perspective and categories involved in varying the responses.

---

## *Exercises in Synthesis and Elaboration*

---

"Briefly, the abilities believed to be most relevant for creative thinking are in two categories. One category is divergent production abilities. . . . The other potential source of creative talents is in the category of 'transformation' abilities, which pertain to revising what one experiences or knows, thereby producing new forms and patterns."

J. P. Guilford

## 73. MAKING UP A STORY
*Objective:*
**To acquire skill in synthesizing and elaborating already existing elements.**
*Resources:*
A trained facilitator.
A set of photographs.

a. The facilitator provides a set of pictures, taken from magazines or photo files, preferably with some people in them. The number of pictures should be several times the number of participants, so that each person has many options to choose from. Participants are asked to select a picture which stirs some feeling in them, either of attraction or of distaste, and to make up a story about it.
b. Form small groups of four to eight persons to share the stories.
c. Discuss:

- What helped to produce ideas? what hindered?
- Which stories were most detailed?
- Which were most original?

d. An alternative exercise: Try a dramatic reading as a starting point, using a scene from a novel, play or short story, with a narrator and the various characters presenting briefly an initial situation. Each participant then writes an ending to the story.

## 74. BRAINSTORMING
*Objective:*
**To learn the technique of brainstorming.**
*Resources:*
A trained facilitator.

a. The facilitator explains the concept and technique of brainstorming:

- The purpose is to generate a profusion of ideas.
- The production of ideas can be improved if certain conditions are met, namely:

1. a group effort—two heads are better than one;
2. a free and open atmosphere which favors spontaneity;
3. a scrupulous avoidance of judging anyone's contribution during the generating process.

- A recorder lists the contributions on newsprint.
- Members try to build on each other's ideas, using them as stimuli or starting points.
- When the brainstorming period is over, the ideas are grouped and evaluated in terms of their usefulness for the project at hand.

b. The task to brainstorm: Suppose I were to be dropped off in the wilderness. What would I need to survive for a weekend? What would be the absolute minimum on which I could manage? (Or the group can choose a current problem.)
c. One member or the facilitator can serve as observer, to call the group on any evaluative language that creeps in during the generating process.
d. Be sure to complete the evaluative phase, selecting from the list the minimum necessities for the survival of one individual on his or her own.

---

*Adapted from E. Paul Torrance, *Torrance Tests of Creative Thinking.* Personnel Press, Inc., Princeton, N.J., 1966.

## 75. CONSTRUCTING A GAME

*Objective:*

**To use brainstorming as an aid in synthesizing.**

a. Divide the group into teams of four or five persons each.

b. The task is to construct a game that can be played with some common object—e.g., a ball, a cup, a rope, the pentaminoes of exercise 62 above—using brainstorming in arriving at a solution.

The group may add additional conditions if they think that will aid the process, e.g., the number of players, the place, the age level, whether it is to be competitive or not, etc.

c. Each team instructs the group in its game and plays the game.

d. Participants vote for the best game.

e. Discuss:

- Did many of the teams have similar ideas?
- Were participants able to build on each other's ideas?
- What helped, what hindered the process of construction?

## 76. WRITING A POEM

*Objective:*

**To write a poem, relying on one's own power to see the world.**

"Children have a natural talent for writing poetry, and anyone who teaches them should know that," writes Kenneth Koch. "Teaching really is not the right word for what takes place: it is more like permitting the children to discover something they already have." Koch has been remarkably successful in helping many people to discover their talent for writing poetry, people who have never thought of themselves as poets—children in elementary schools, old people in nursing homes. The purpose is "to encourage people to be free and deep and extravagant in what they write so that they could find what was hidden in themselves that they had to say."

In the excerpt below from *Wishes, Lies and Dreams,* Koch describes some of the methods he uses with children. They would apply equally well to anyone interested in getting in touch with the poet in oneself. Other suggestions can be found in his books, *I Never Told Anybody* and *Rose, Where Did You Get That Red?*

a. Here are some of the starting points Koch has used that you might like to try:

- Think about your wishes, real wishes as wild and crazy as you like, and begin every line with "I wish . . ."
- Look at some object in the room—your hand, a sheet of paper, a piece of chalk—and compare it to something which is like it in only one way. Write a comparison poem, using "like" or "as" in every line.
- Put a lie in every line or make up a whole poem in which nothing is true.
- Associate colors freely with all kinds of things—sounds, places, words, numbers—and write a poem with a color in every line, the same color or different colors or different shades of the same color.
- Think of differences between your past and present self and begin alternate lines with "I used to. . ." and "But now. . ." or with "I used to be. . ." and "But now I am. . ." or with "I used to think. . ." and "But now I know. . ."
- With eyes closed, listen to music for a few minutes. You may want to associate the music with sounds, colors, places, times of the year, feelings of happiness or sadness. Write whatever the music makes you think of.
- Think of how you appear to others and how you seem to yourself and begin alternate lines with "I seem to be. . ." and "But really I am. . ."
- Think of some object that interests or excites you—the rain, the river, a piece of pottery, an animal, or whatever—and write as if you were that object.

b. To put yourself in the mood for writing, it is often helpful to read some poems aloud. Here is a poem written by a seventh grader, who was inspired by Wallace Stevens' "Thirteen Ways of Looking at a Blackbird."

## *Five Ways of Looking at a Pond*

A pond is just a mirror
    left alone, amongst the grasses
    to reflect the sky
A single tear from skies above
    finally cooled
    by evening winds
A shiny silver button
    dropped from a giant's coat
    never to be found
Made of green jade
    a chinese bowl
    surrounded by leafy, green temples

Blue paint accidentally dribbled
   on the green carpet
   of a hill.

—Molly Hankwitz, 7th Grade in Koch, *Rose, Where Did You Get That Red?* p. 125

c. If you are working in a group, read the poems aloud.

## 77. ROLE PLAYING SPECIFIC SITUATIONS

*Objective:*

**To enable participants to imagine and act out alternative forms of behavior.**

*Resources:*
A trained facilitator.

a. The facilitator can propose situations appropriate to the age and experience of the group, for example:

- young person asking parent for use of the family car;
- young person returning home late to find mother waiting up;
- family of four or five people with different interests planning a family vacation;
- student asking for a change of grade from a teacher.

b. Situations can be derived from the experiences of members of the group. Small groups can brainstorm recent incidents that they wish had turned out differently.
c. After a situation is chosen, allow a few minutes for the players to feel their way into their roles and set the scene. Within the limits of the situation (e.g., the father is unwilling to let his seventeen-year-old son take the family car on a date), encourage the players to define the character as they wish.

Make use of alter egos: When someone in the group thinks of an alternative response, he or she can come forward, put a hand on the shoulder of the speaker, and voice the alternative.

Make use of role reversal—when the scene is finished, the person who played the parent takes the role of the child, etc.
d. Discuss:

- How many alternative ways could each party respond to the situation?
- What are the probable results of the various responses?

## 78. LIFE PLANNING*
*Note:*

This exercise requires a good deal of time—at least six to eight hours, preferably divided into three or four sessions with several days in between, so that participants can approach each set of exercises with fresh energies. Participants should save the materials generated in the exercises, as each session builds upon materials produced earlier.

*Objectives:*

**To enable participants to envisage possible futures for themselves.**

**To enable participants to clarify and prioritize broad life goals.**

**To enable participants to develop concrete projects that combine several of these future priority goals.**

### Part I: Where Am I Now?

a. Life line.

- Draw your life line, using the left edge of the paper to represent life's beginning and the right edge its end, and making a check mark to indicate where you are now.
- Form triads, share and discuss your drawings:

1. Why did you draw your line as you did?
2. Where are the most significant turning points in your line?
3. Where are the most important decisions made by yourself?

- Reflect and note down for yourself anything that you learn about yourself from this sharing.

b. Identifying some personal life goals.
Below is an alphabetical list of broad life goals:
   affection—to obtain and share companionship and affection
   duty—to dedicate myself to what I call duty
   expertness—to become an authority in some field
   independence—to have freedom of thought and action
   leadership—to become influential
   parenthood—to raise a family, to have heirs
   pleasure—to enjoy life, to be happy and contented
   power—to have control of others
   prestige—to become well known
   security—to have a secure and stable position
   self-realization—to optimize my personal development

---

*Adapted from George A. Ford and Gordon Lippitt: *Planning Your Future.* University Associates, La Jolla, Cal., 1972.

service—to contribute to the welfare of others
wealth—to earn a great deal of money

- Rank this list in terms of your own values from (1) for most important to (13) for least important. Do this quickly, in terms of your first reactions; then go back and review your rankings, changing them if necessary.
- Goals can vary, both in their clarity and in the degree of commitment we have toward them. Here is a four-point scale:

1. High clarity—high commitment
(I know where I want to go and I'm eager to get there.)
2. High clarity—low commitment
(I know where I'm supposed to go, but I don't want to.)
3. Low clarity—high commitment
(I want to do something, but I'm not sure what.)
4. Low clarity—low commitment
(I don't feel like doing anything and I don't care.)

Review your five top priorities and evaluate them in terms of the above four-point scale.

- Jot down two or three small first steps you could take now to move you toward your goals.
- Share your results with your triad.

c. Who am I now?

- On twenty slips of paper, jot down twenty responses to the question: "Who am I?" Be spontaneous; use any of the ways you think about yourself—your roles, skills, characteristics, relationships, etc.
- Sort your statements into three groups: positive, negative, and neutral.
- Share with your triad.
- Note down for yourself any discoveries you have made about yourself.

## Part II: Where Do I Want To Be?

a. Fantasizing a future.

- Write a brief biography of yourself, two or three paragraphs as you would like to see them, toward the end of your life, in a *Who's Who* or at a testimonial dinner.
- Write a sketch of an ideal day or two in your life in the relatively near future, say in two to five years from now. Where will you be? with whom? doing what? how will you feel about your life?
- Exchange statements with the members of your triad. Each person takes the statements of one other and looks for the goals that are explicit or

implicit therein. Write down and share with each other.

- Compare these goals with your five top priorities from I-b above. They should be fairly consistent; if not, reconsider your choices and revise.

b. Who would I like to be?

- Think of your work or career and write eight or ten statements of attainments you would like to achieve.
- Do the same for your relationships.
- Do the same for your personal satisfactions.
- Rank each of the items on the above three lists according to the following four-point scale:

1. not important.
2. somewhat important.
3. of great importance.
4. of highest importance.

- Make a list of the six items of highest importance and the six of least importance.
- Share with your triad.

c. Life inventory

- Jot down your responses to the following categories as quickly and spontaneously as you can. Overlaps and duplications do not matter.

1. Peak experiences I have had—great moments when I felt really alive.
2. Things I would like to learn to do well either because I must or because I want to.
3. Things I would like to stop doing—family, friends, co-workers might have suggestions.
4. Peak experiences I would like to have.
5. Things I would like to start doing now (note these down just as they come to your mind; don't censor anything).

- Share with your triad.
- Compare your list of things you would like to do now with your five top priority life goals from Part I-b and with your six top items in who you would like to be from Part II-b. Are your action steps reasonably consistent with your goals? If not, you may want to reconsider and try to locate the causes of the discrepancies.

## Part III: Developing Some Concrete Projects

A general strategy: You need not devise a separate project for every goal you have in mind. Try to combine several goals in one concrete project. Also try to find others who share your goals and are willing to join with you in some of your projects.

a. Review your highest priority items and jot them down. Be sure to include:

- your three highest broad life goals
- your small first steps to action
- your three top "Who I want to be"
- three long range goals from your autobiography
- the peak experiences you would like to have
- the things you would like to start doing now

b. By combining some of these goals, desires and actions, make at least three concrete projects for yourself. For instance, "I want to earn money for school, I want to test out a career choice, I want to deepen a relationship with a friend. So I'm going to look for a summer job in my field in my friend's home town."

c. Review your lowest priorities and jot them down. Be sure to include:

- your three lowest life goals
- the three things you would most like to stop doing
- your three lowest "Who I'd like to be"

d. Combine these into projects you can drop from your agenda for the time being to make room for your highest priorities.

---

# Solutions

## EXERCISE 57.

**START**

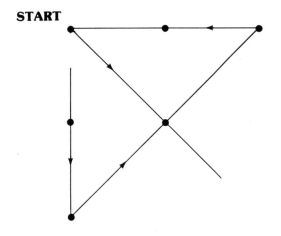

## EXERCISE 59.
### a. Redefine:
Not how do we get the barrels onto the scale, but how do we determine the freight charges? Weigh samples of standard sizes. Or use a roadside weigh station, weighing the empty and the loaded truck.
### b. Redefine:
How to get the job done satisfactorily? Provide training for the employee; or discuss his difficulties to get at the cause; shift him to other work for which he is better suited and hire a replacement; review the job descriptions and reassign some elements of the task to other jobs, etc.

### c. Redefine:
In what other ways could she help the group reach its goals? Could she do other, less time-consuming work for the group, thus freeing someone else for the finance job? Or could she find another person to undertake the job? Or do it with a co-chairperson?
### d. Redefine:
How can he meet the requirements for graduation? through an alternative course? a special dispensation? Or can he meet the course requirement in an alternative way—through an independent study or a special project?

## EXERCISE 60.
There are thirty squares in the diagram:

| | |
|---|---:|
| • The total square. | 1 |
| • The perimeter of the inside four squares. | 1 |
| • The four quadrants. | 4 |
| • The four sets of nine squares, one from each corner. | 4 |
| • The four sets of four squares, one from each side. | 4 |
| • The sixteen small squares. | 16 |
| **Total** | 30 |

## EXERCISE 61.
2 + 2; 2 × 2; 22; 2/2

# PART VI:
# EXERCISES TO DEVELOP SYSTEMS SKILLS

Each day we must deal with a large number of complex, highly abstract, bureaucratic systems which sustain our society and pattern our behavior. We feel systemic pressure from government agencies, educational institutions, business and industry with their often gigantic national and multinational corporations, from banks, law courts, and transportation networks.

The person who has system skills is not only able to follow the rules and regulations of the various systems of which he or she is a part but can exercise more advanced skills. He or she is able to think of the system as a whole, identify the parts, understand how these parts interrelate, and communicate those understandings. He or she is able to make judgments about the worth of the system and has the skill to intervene to make the necessary changes. People in leadership positions—those having responsibility for structuring an organization, developing policies and procedures—need well-developed systems skills.

Clearly, system skills require adequate development and integration of the other three sets of skills. Coping with the day to day problems of getting along in the system may require instrumental skills, such as the ability to fill out the necessary forms or to locate the right person to call in an emergency. One may even employ imaginal skills in figuring out how to take advantage of the system in small ways. For example, most college students learn how to deal with the registration system to get the classes they want or how to deal with the housing office to secure a desirable room. Or a welfare recipient may know where to go and how to proceed to obtain certain kinds of aid. But these coping skills do not qualify as full system skills as we are using the term.

This section is not necessarily intended to prepare you to become president of General Motors but simply to help you make a start on a set of skills that are important for survival and achievement in the modern world and that take a lifetime to develop fully.

## 79. TIME MANAGEMENT

One basic method of improving the way in which we accomplish what we intend is to manage time. If we are constantly under pressure to complete tasks, it leaves less energy for other areas of development. All of us can profit by a systematic approach to time management.

*Objective:*
**To develop a time management strategy for completing a task.**

a. Select a task that you must complete by a certain date. Examples might be: writing a term paper, giving a party, painting the house, or making a sales presentation.

b. List all the things that must be done (subtasks) before the task is completed.

|  |  |
|---|---|
| 1. | 3. |
| 2. | 4. |
| 5. | 9. |
| 6. | 10. |
| 7. | 11. |
| 8. | 12. |

c. For each subtask, decide how long each will take and decide by when each one must be completed.

d. Find a large calendar. Draw lines on the calendar to represent each subtask and the time it will take to complete it. Start first with those subtasks which have a firm starting or finishing date; then add others, taking care that you do not have too many things to do all at once.

   By creating a series of due dates, you have created an orderly system for getting the job done without going through the pressure and confusion of the last minute rush.

e. Review your schedule again, this time noting other possible time conflicts which might arise from your work, school, family or other commitments or opportunities. Shift your task completion schedule as necessary.

f. Share your ideas and observations with a partner or in a small group.

*(Example)*
*Task:*

To write a paper which is due December 3. Assignment given September 15.

*Subtask list:*
Choose topic
Search for resources
Draft outline
Research
Revise outline
Submit outline (Due October 8)
Write introduction
Write first draft
Revise draft
Type paper
Proofread paper
Hand in paper—9:00 A.M. December 3

## SEPTEMBER

| S | M | T | W | T | F | S |
|---|---|---|---|---|---|---|
| | | | 1 | 2 | 3 | 4 |
| 5 | 6 | 7 | 8 | 9 | 10 | 11 |
| 12 | 13 | 14 | 15 | 16 | 17 | 18 Choose |
| 19 topic for paper | 20 | 21 | 22 | 23 | 24 Resources | 25 |
| 26 | 27 | 28 Draft outline Research time | 29 | 30 | | |

## OCTOBER

| S | M | T | W | T | F | S |
|---|---|---|---|---|---|---|
| | | | | | 1 Research | 2 |
| 3 time | 4 | 5 Revise outline | 6 | 7 | 8 Submit outline | 9 |
| 10 | 11 | 12 Research time | 13 | 14 | 15 Weekend | 16 |
| 17 Guests | 18 | 19 Write introduction | 20 | 21 Write first draft | 22 | 23 |
| 24 | 25 | 26 | 27 (Study for mid-term exams) | 28 | 29 | 30 |
| 31 | | | | | | |

## NOVEMBER

| S | M | T | W | T | F | S |
|---|---|---|---|---|---|---|
|  | 1 | 2 | 3 | 4 | 5 | 6 |
|  |  |  | (Midterm exams week) |  |  | PARTY! |
| 7 | 8 | 9 | 10 | 11 | 12 | 13 |
|  |  |  | Revise draft |  |  |  |
| 14 | 15 | 16 | 17 | 18 | 19 | 20 |
|  | Type paper |  |  | (Out of town trip— |  |  |
| 21 | 22 | 23 | 24 | 25 | 26 | 27 |
|  | Out of town) |  |  |  | Proofread paper |  |
| 28 | 29 | 30 |  |  |  |  |
|  | Make last |  |  |  |  |  |

## DECEMBER

| S | M | T | W | T | F | S |
|---|---|---|---|---|---|---|
|  |  |  | 1 | 2 | 3 |  |
|  |  |  | Changes |  | Submit paper |  |

## 80. DEVELOPING A BUDGET SYSTEM

Another starting point for building system skills is the development of your ability to handle money. Not only is this an important skill, and an essential aspect of any system, but it is also a process which can be revealing with respect to your value development. Your decisions about spending money are reflections of your choices about what is important.

*Objective:*

### To practice financial management skills.

a. Spend about ten minutes listing all the expenses you have had over the past few months. Do not be concerned over the amount paid; just list the items. You might come up with things such as:

| | |
|---|---|
| shoes | gas |
| party supplies | tires |
| rent | theater tickets |
| insurance | school supplies |
| club dues | tuition |
| food | toothpaste |
| haircut | parking fees |
| dry cleaning | overdue book fines |

b. Now decide which items are fixed and which are flexible. Fixed items are those for which periodic and prearranged payment is due such as rent and tuition. Flexible items are those which you buy from time to time and over which you have more control in terms of when you will buy them and what they will cost. Circle those which are fixed.

c. Based on your recall of your main items of expense, you are now prepared to make a budget projection for the coming month or months. Develop a worksheet such as the one below, adjusting it for your situation.

Month of _____

| Estimated income | | Estimated expenses | |
|---|---|---|---|
| Cash on hand | $_____ | Fixed expenses | |
| Salary/wages | _____ | Insurance | $_____ |
| Interest/dividends | _____ | Tuition | _____ |
| Gifts | _____ | Rent | _____ |
| Other | _____ | Utilities | _____ |
| | | **Flexible expenses** | |
| | | Food | _____ |
| | | Entertainment | _____ |
| | | Gas | _____ |
| | | Etc. | _____ |
| Total | $_____ | Total | $_____ |

Income $_____ equals expenses $_____ plus savings $_____

d. In order to improve your ability to predict expenses, you might construct a ledger such as the one following which keeps track of your daily expenses. Monthly or quarterly summaries should be made. With a clear idea of your existing spending pattern, you should be able to make a decision about setting priorities based on your income and your goals.

*(Example)*

| Income for month $_____ | Daily Expense Record<br>Cash on hand first day<br>of month $_____   c | | | | | | | | Month of _____ | |
|---|---|---|---|---|---|---|---|---|---|---|
| *Expenses* | 1 | 2 | 3 | 4 | 5 | 6 | 7 | 8 | 9 | 10 |
| 1. Food | | | | | | | | | | |
| 2. Rent | | | | | | | | | | |
| 3. Utilities | | | | | | | | | | |
| 4. Etc. | | | | | | | | | | |

## 81. YOU AND YOUR SYSTEMS

Improving your system skills depends on your ability to analyze the systems in which you are now participating. Any system is a complex whole with interacting parts, each of which may be studied as a separate subsystem or as a set of interrelationships. As a first step it is useful to be aware of the many systems of which you are a part.

*Objective:*

**To become more aware of the various systems in which you are now functioning.**

a. List at least ten systems in which you are now participating along with your particular role in each. To help generate ideas, trace your path through your daily activities or look inside your wallet or purse!

| *System* | *My Role* |
|---|---|
| 1. bus system | 1. rider |
| 2. family | 2. son/daughter |
| 3. _____ | 3. _____ |
| 4. _____ | 4. _____ |
| 5. _____ | 5. _____ |
| 6. _____ | 6. _____ |
| 7. _____ | 7. _____ |
| 8. _____ | 8. _____ |
| 9. _____ | 9. _____ |
| 10. _____ | 10. _____ |

b. Compare your list with a partner's.
c. Check your system list against ours on page 139.

# 82. SEEING THE SYSTEM

Now that you have identified some systems in your life, let's analyze one of them to discover how many parts it contains.

*Objective:*

**To identify the various parts of a given system.**

a. Select one of the systems identified in exercise 81.
b. List all the parts you can think of.

*(Example)*

**System:** Bus System
**Parts:** Bus driver, roads, routing schedule, repair service, gas or electricity sources, manufacturer, advertisers, designer of interior, insurance, technical designer, legal department, company management, payroll, transportation as a service value, safety, fare rates.

System: _____

Parts: _____
_____
_____

c. Arrange the elements of your system under the following categories.

1. Purposes, aims, functions
2. Basic resources used
3. Technology (machinery/skills)
4. Personnel (Who does the work?)
5. Finance (How does the system get started? keep going?)
6. Legal aspects
7. Management structure (organizational chart)
8. Aesthetic considerations
9. Health and environmental considerations

Do you have any elements that do not fit the nine categories? Any categories without system parts?

d. Share and discuss with a partner or small group.

# 83. ANALYZING SYSTEMS

Marvin R. Weisbord's *Organizational Diagnosis* (Addison Wesley, 1978) provides an excellent model for seeing an institution, an organization or any of its parts as a system. He includes the following categories in his approach:

1. *Boundaries.* We need to decide what is included inside our system and where to draw a line beyond which we shall not analyze. Those forces, people, units, and organizations which have impact on our particular system but over which we have little control are called the environment.

2. *Input/Output.* Our system receives resources from the outside environment, changes or transforms them in some way and then sends the products out into the environment. One can see, for example, a bicycle repair shop at work taking in damaged machines, fixing them and sending them out to customers.

3. *Purposes of the organization.* By purposes, Weisbord means the organization's current agenda including what it wants to accomplish while also acknowledging its limitations. Purposes should define the organization's uniqueness, that is, what it does that others do not do.

4. *Structure.* Structure refers to the "organization chart" which describes the division of labor and the lines of authority in your system.

5. *Relationships.* Relationships include not only reference to the ways in which people either cooperate or conflict, but also the ways people interact with the technology in your system. It can, in large systems, also refer to the way units interact with each other.

6. *Rewards.* Every system has both formal and informal rewards, ranging from simple monetary gain to the more subtle aspects of job satisfaction and quality of interpersonal relationships.

7. *Leadership.* Leadership is, of course, needed to insure that the system continues to function well.

8. *Helpful Mechanisms.* Weisbord uses this category to remind us of the need to invent ways of coordinating functions, to increase efficiency and to eliminate routines, habits and procedures which get in the way.

Let's apply his model to something with which we are all familiar: the classroom. As a first step, we need to define our territory, that is, what is inside our system and what is outside. A classroom has students, teachers, physical space, equipment and furniture. But outside of the classroom itself are a number of things which support or are in other ways related to the classroom. Some of them include: library, bursar, film center, legislative decisions and electrical energy sources.

## LIST OF SYSTEMS: Ex. 81

| System | My Role |
|---|---|
| Business | Employee, customer |
| | Student |
| School, College | Voter, office-holder, taxpayer |
| Political System | Consumer of service |
| Police Department | Patient |
| Hospital | Member |
| Team | Member of congregation |
| Church | Office holder |
| Club | Private |
| Committee | Member |
| Armed Forces | Contract signer, defendant |
| Legal System | Receiver of benefits |
| Social Security | Payer of premiums |
| Insurance | Consumer |
| Utilities | Borrower, saver |
| Banking System | User |
| Credit Card System | Viewer |
| Television | Borrower |
| Library | You as manager |
| Your Body | You as nourisher or destroyer |
| Ecological System | |

The circle of relationships is certainly wide and complex. Can you think of others to include in this list?

_____

_____

_____

_____

Weisbord then invites us to look at our classroom system in terms of inputs, process and outputs. Resources are coming into the system, being changed in some way and then sent out again into the world beyond our system boundary as products, services or ideas.

| *Inputs* | *Outputs* |
|---|---|
| Ideas of students | New ideas |
| Ideas of teachers | New knowledge |
| Experience of students | New skills and techniques |
| Experience of teachers | New value stances |
| Materials | Products (papers, art-work, projects) |
| Skills and techniques | |
| Values | |

We also must establish a feedback loop from outputs back to inputs. Such an evaluation component may include examinations, teacher evaluations, or evaluations of papers and projects. The data gathered can then be used to decide what changes might be made in the "process" or "transformation" or what changes might be made in the selection of inputs.

Now let's take a closer look at the transformation process, that is, the actual activity or behavior in the classroom. We can use the following analytic categories: purposes, structure, relationships, rewards, leadership and helpful mechanisms.

*Purpose.* In our classroom, the teacher and the students need to decide why they are there, and what they intend to accomplish in any given time frame. These decisions are usually called educational goals and objectives. You might decide, for example, that your original mission of teaching/learning biology might be better expressed as the discovery of truth about living things. Whatever you decide, you ought to at least think about your purposes and not just assume that what you are going to learn or teach is always going to involve the best use of your time and energy. Thinking carefully about purposes involves a reflection on your own values and on what you consider worthwhile for yourself and/or for others. And remember, if you do not know where you are going the chances are good that you will wind up somewhere else!

*Structure.* The usual diagram of classroom structure looks like this:

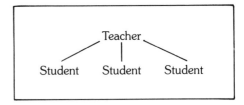

But you may find that there are other kinds of arrangements which will better equip you to achieve your goals. These might include discussion groups, project teams, or simulations. There also may be team teaching or a graduate assistant involved. Your structure should "fit" the purposes.

*Relationships.* One way to categorize personal relationships within an organization is in terms of interdependence. How much cooperation is needed to accomplish class objectives? Cooperation for its own sake, while desirable, may not be appropriate to one's individual sense of personal achievement. Unnecessary competition, on the other hand, may set a tone of mutual distrust and hostility. Two main considerations should be kept in mind: relationships are good to the extent that they carry forward the organization's purposes and that they add to or maintain the self-esteem of individuals. Elsewhere, we have discussed the development of values within individuals and noted that value development varies widely among individuals. While some class members are ready to skillfully engage in cooperative efforts for the rewards of creativity, others are still concerned about individual recognition. Care must be taken to insure that relationships allow all to grow and are not producing destructive conflicts among members of the group.

*Rewards.* In most classrooms, teacher praise and grades seem to be the most important rewards. Other factors, however, may be at work as we have noticed in the preceding section. Peer approval, personal satisfaction in creative work, a sense of contribution to the society at large and other rewards may be significant. In any case, a system must take into account rewards for individuals within it if the system is to be effective.

*Leadership.* The leader, manager or teacher insures the fit among all other aspects of the system. He or she systematically monitors the purposes, human relationships, rewards/incentives and organizational structures so that maximum output is achieved. Current management theory now stresses the desirability of a consultative or shared style of leadership but does not suggest that leadership is no longer important. Any system must develop its appropriate leadership style to fit its purposes.

*Helpful mechanisms.* A helpful mechanism in a classroom might be a periodic class/teacher review of objectives and learning strategies to enable corrective action to be taken during the course. A dysfunctional mechanism might be the furniture which cannot be moved easily to facilitate class discussion or group work on projects.

Now it's your turn.

*Objective:*

**To apply the Weisbord model to a system.**

a. Select a system in which you are currently participating.

b. Follow the outline below in describing the system.

1. Boundaries
2. Inputs/outputs
3. The six parts of the system:

- Purposes
- Structure
- Relationships
- Rewards
- Leadership
- Helpful mechanisms

c. Share with partner or small group. It is helpful for the group to be part of the same or a similar kind of system.

## 84. DEVELOPING VISION ABOUT SYSTEMS CHANGE

How do we improve on the human environment? How do we make our systems work better for us? A first step requires getting an idea of what we want to see happen, making value judgments about what is *good* and making an assessment about the direction of change we want to encourage.

If we assume that humans are going to be happier, more productive, and fulfilled, when they are functioning at phases III and IV, we have a vision of what direction we want for ourselves and for others. (Your analysis and valuing decisions may of course indicate a different vision of the good life.) The following exercise is an illustration of applying a value vision to a system.

*Objective:*

**To practice vision in thinking about systems change.**

*Resources:* Classroom organization chart. (See Work Sheet Ex. 84.)

a. Distribute copies of classroom organization chart to group members.

b. Each person should circle the blocks which reflects the best situation in which he or she would

like to participate and be able to state a reason for the choice.

c. Discuss in small groups.

d. Optional—Discuss the application of Brian Hall's Phases of Consciousness to the categories used to evaluate classrooms.

e. Choose another system situation and construct an evaluation instrument using appropriate categories.

## 85. GROUP DISCUSSION AS SYSTEM

A common example of a system that would appear not to have a well defined structure yet in which we participate quite often is a group discussion. Here our focus is less on division of labor, and more on the process of human interaction taking place. Although many group discussions are formed and disbanded spontaneously at the will of the group, nevertheless there is a set of interrelationships which can be analyzed as a system. And if you can understand how the system works, you can improve it by playing your role effectively.

*Objectives:*

**To learn the differences between process and content.**

**To learn the roles people play in group discussion.**

**To make decisions about changing one's role in group discussion.**

a. Form a discussion group inside a circle of observers (fishbowl or group on group model).

X = observer          O = discussion group member

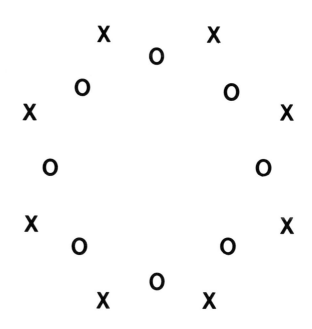

# FOUR TYPES OF CLASSROOM ORGANIZATION: EX. 84

| | A | B | C | D |
|---|---|---|---|---|
| How much confidence is shown in students? | Very little | Some | Substantial amount | A great deal |
| How free do they feel to talk to the teacher? | Not very free | Somewhat free | Rather free | Very free |
| Is predominant use made of 1) fear, 2) threats, 3) punishments, 4) rewards, 5) involvement? | 1, 2, 3, occasionally 4 | 4, some 3 | 4, some 3 and 5 | 5, 4 based on group set goals |
| How candid is communication? | Very cautious | Quite cautious | Often candid | Usually candid |
| What is the direction of information flow? | Downward (teacher to student) | Mostly downward | Down and up | Down, up and sideways |
| How well does the teacher know problems faced by individual students? | Knows little | Some knowledge | Accurate but limited | Very accurate |
| What is the basis for decision making? | School policy exclusively | School policy and teacher judgment | School policy, teacher judg-ment—some stu-dent consideration | By teacher and students within school policy |
| Are students involved in decisions related to their classroom obligations? | Not very often | Occasionally consulted | Generally consulted | Fully involved |
| How are classroom organizational goals established? | Directions given by teacher | Teacher direction, some opportunity for comment by students | After discussion, teacher decides | By group decision as a rule |
| How is classroom performance reviewed and evaluated? | Almost always by teacher alone | Teacher listens to student, but makes evaluation alone | Evaluation somewhat shared by teacher | Evaluation widely shared by teacher and student |
| What are test scores and other control data used for? | Keep student in line, punish for failure | Keep student in line, reward and punishment | Control through reward and some self-guidance | Largely for self-direction and problem solving |

# Content Observer Sheet: Ex. 85a

| List topics or General Areas of Discussion: | What terms or concepts were introduced? Were they clarified? | | | What issues were introduced? Were they clarified? | | |
|---|---|---|---|---|---|---|
| | Terms (Identify below) | Clarified? (Place "x") | | Issues (Identify below) | Clarified? (Place "x") | |
| | | Yes | No | | Yes | No |
| | | | | | | |
| | | | | | | |
| | | | | | | |
| | | | | | | |
| | | | | | | |
| | | | | | | |
| | | | | | | |

Tally the number of each of the following by recording "x's" as the discussion progresses.

| | Total |
|---|---|
| Relevant supporting examples given: | |
| Sources of information identified: | |
| Cogent argument presented: | |

Did the group stay on the topic? Yes _____ No _____ Comment:

In general, were the arguments logically presented? Yes _____ No _____ Comment:

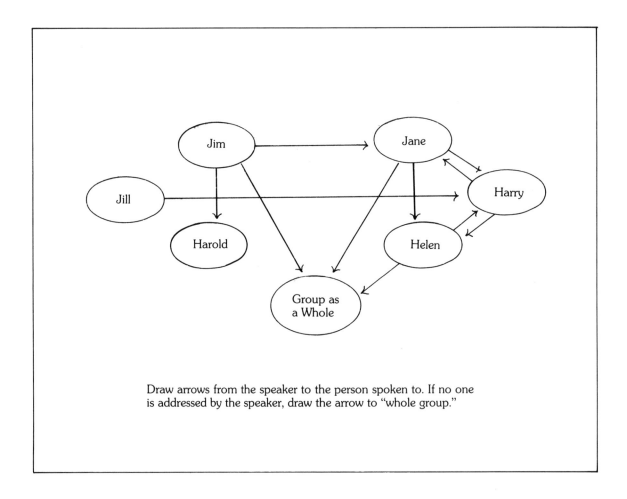

Draw arrows from the speaker to the person spoken to. If no one is addressed by the speaker, draw the arrow to "whole group."

Alternative to the Observer Sheet: Use a ball of string and individually hold pencils. In order to speak, one must hold the ball of string and then wind it once or twice around his or her pencil. As the discussion continues, the unwinding ball will pattern the flow of conversation.

# Role Observer Sheet: Ex. 85c

Below are listed various roles played by group discussion participants. They include "Gate Keeper" who encourages others to speak; "Tail Gater" who agrees with what has just been said; "Initiator" who originates a line of discussion; "Summarizer" who summarizes or clarifies; "Group Maintainer" who gives supporting comments or relieves tension by a joke; "Blocker" who shuts off discussion, interrupts or diverts group attention; and "Task Director" who keeps the group on the topic or reminds the group of time remaining.

Place a check mark along with an occasional explanatory note to yourself indicating roles assumed by the individuals identified along the top of the chart.

|  | Jane | Jim | Harold | Helen | Harry | Jill |
|---|---|---|---|---|---|---|
| Gate Keeper |  |  |  |  |  |  |
| Tail Gater |  |  |  |  |  |  |
| Initiator |  |  |  |  |  |  |
| Summarizer |  |  |  |  |  |  |
| Group Maintainer |  |  |  |  |  |  |
| Blocker |  |  |  |  |  |  |
| Task Director |  |  |  |  |  |  |

b. Choose a topic for discussion such as a moral or political issue or a planning task.

c. Distribute among the observers one of three observer check lists ("Content," "Process," or "Roles." (Cf. Ex. 85a, 85b, 85c.)

d. Discuss the topic for an agreed upon length of time.

e. Invite the observers to comment on the group's performance.

f. Discuss:

- How did the people in the group feel about what happened? about their roles?
- What were the advantages and disadvantages of the various roles people assumed?

g. Reverse the groups with the former discussants now acting as observers. Choose a topic which is of a similar nature to the one just discussed.

h. Reflect on your own role in group discussion and then share with others. How could group discussion be improved?

## 86. DEALING WITH SYSTEMS: AUTHORITY

There is a certain gentle art one must learn in dealing with human systems so that they work for you and not against you. Businesses, for example, are supposed to provide services and products at reasonable costs. But what if you are overcharged or receive shoddy merchandise? What should you do if, in your work place, your boss keeps asking you to do extra work as a personal favor but he or she does not offer any additional pay? What do you do if an instructor gives you a surprisingly low grade on a paper which you feel was well written?

Many people have turned to "assertiveness" as a technique which allows your own power as a person to work constructively for you. Being assertive is the art of conducting yourself in such a way that you are neither a passive doormat, denying your own rights (non-assertive), nor a ranting, obnoxious person who tramples on the rights of others (aggressive).

*Objective:*

**To recognize the difference between non-assertive, assertive, and aggressive behavior.**

a. Assume you have been overcharged on your tuition fee at your college. You dropped a course, but you are still being billed as if you continued in the course, and you are sure you were within the time limit allowed for cancellation. Below are some possible responses you might make. Next

to each, in the space provided, place a letter which indicates one of the following:

N - non-assertive behavior
A - assertive behavior
G - aggressive behavior

_____ 1. Call home and tell your family about the tyranny of the college bursar.

_____ 2. Call your lawyer and prepare for a lawsuit.

_____ 3. Demand that the clerk in the bursar's office fix the error immediately or you will go directly to the president with the case.

_____ 4. Go to the president's office and complain about the gross inefficiency of the bursar's office.

_____ 5. Call for an appointment to see the bursar and present your problem.

_____ 6. Write a letter to the bursar in which you include xeroxed copies of relevant transactions and ask that you receive a new bill.

_____ 7. Send off a quick note to the university academic accrediting agency about your case with a copy to the bursar to insure quick action.

_____ 8. Wait for a while to see if the college corrects its mistake.

b. If you have designated responses 1 and 8 as non-assertive, 5 and 6 as assertive, and 2, 3, 4, and 7 as aggressive, you are getting the idea! Note that response 1 is misdirected energy and is an avoidance behavior. Note also that the aggressive responses either impose unnecessarily on others' time or threaten other people without justification. Such behavior also creates enemies for yourself very rapidly!

c. Try to think of other assertive approaches you might use in this situation.

d. Discuss your ideas with a partner or within a small group.

## 87. APPLYING ASSERTIVENESS

Remember that assertiveness involves at the outset a change of attitude about yourself as a person. As a human being you have a basic set of rights and responsibilities with respect to others. In our culture, they include:

1. command over your time, your property and your body.

2. the right to express your opinion; to express yourself.

3. the right to be respected as a person.

4. the right to refuse a request.
5. the right to ask for things that you need.
6. the right to question those in authority.
7. the right to be angry with others.

You should also give yourself the freedom

1. to be wrong on occasion.
2. to not have to justify every action to other people.
3. to be less than perfect in your work.
4. not to be liked by everyone.

*Objective:*
### To gain skills in assertive behavior.

a. Describe in writing a situation in which you did not act with assertiveness or a situation that is coming up soon in which assertiveness would be useful.
b. Choose a partner and an observer.
c. Role play the situation with your partner. The observer should keep track of non-assertive, assertive, and aggressive elements.
d. Discuss.
e. Change roles and repeat.

*Note:* Many people become afraid when faced with authority figures. It is useful therefore to distinguish between *rational* anxiety, rationalization, and irrational thought. "What if he fires me?" and "It probably won't do any good anyway" are examples of irrational thinking and rationalization. Try to face a situation realistically and make some rational judgments about what will be the probable effect of your acting assertively. Usually, an assertive person will, by his or her behavior, produce a favorable reaction from others simply because his or her behavior is viewed as appropriate *and* legitimate.

## 88. IDENTIFYING GROUP VALUES

Each of us belongs to one or more groups, be they professional, social or community based. As John Geiger explains in Chapter 14 of *Readings in Value De-*velopment, each group represents, whether stated or unstated, a set of values. Groups, moreover, often are regarded by others as having certain value positions or standing for something of value. For example, the medical profession is associated with the value of human life and of healing even though a given doctor may not be motivated by such high ideals all the time. Some groups may be quite aware of their value positions and make explicit statements, using codes of ethics, objectives and purposes, preambles to constitutions and the like.

*Objective:*
### To recognize the values that are operative within an organized group.

a. Choose a specific group to which several people in the room now belong.
b. Review the material in Chapter 14 of *Readings.*
c. Write three or four reasons for the existence of the group in the first place.
d. Write down some ideas that other people outside the group have about what the group is doing.
e. Examine any formal statements of ethics or purpose that the group has produced.
f. Discuss with your peers the values represented in "c" through "e." Reach a consensus on a list of those values.
g. Now describe five or more recent activities by the group. What values are indicated by these activities? How do these values compare with the values you listed in "f"? Discuss the implications of any inconsistency you discover.
h. Reflect on the values you have identified. Are you yourself satisfied with what you have discovered? Are your values in harmony with those of the group to which you belong?
i. (Optional) Locate your group's values on the Phases and Stages of Consciousness Chart at the end of Part II, p. 69. Compare this with your own chart. Reflect on the similarities and differences you discover.

# APPENDIX

## Learning Summaries

Frequently in books that are used in college courses, you will find several quizzes and exams for teachers to use. In this book we are offering an alternative. It is important for students to be able to make as many choices as possible relative to their learnings. One of the most critical of these choices is that of determining what material is most important and has the most value for the student.

The learning summary provides an opportunity for students to review and reflect on material as a good exam does, but does not involve memorization and regurgitation.

Learning summaries are forms that enable students to reflect upon and respond to each class session. The learning summary review will enable students to re-explore and integrate the material at the end of the term. In addition, the summaries and the review provide both teacher and student with evaluative feedback.

---

### Instructions for Learning Summary:

Indicate the date, the time the class meets and the number of the summary, starting with the number one, for the first day of class, then numbering consecutively throughout the term.

Indicate the major topics and subtopics covered during the class session.

Indicate the significant learnings gained from the material and class session. These learnings should include important facts, ideas and concepts.

### Sample

NAME _____

CLASS TIME _____

NUMBER _____

DATE _____

TOPICS AND SUBTOPICS COVERED

1. _____
2. _____
3. _____
4. _____
5. _____
6. _____
7. _____
8. _____
9. _____
10. _____

LEARNINGS: (Facts, Ideas, Concepts)

1. _____
   _____
2. _____
   _____
3. _____
   _____
4. _____
   _____
5. _____
   _____

6. _____

_____

7. _____

_____

8. _____

_____

9. _____

_____

Indicate how you feel about the material and the class session. Any way you feel is O.K.

Be aware of honestly identifying those feelings.

Your teacher may choose a question that is important to help you think about significant issues raised in the material or during the class session. The instructor may assign that question or a choice of questions to the class. An alternate way to complete this section would be for you to identify a significant question for yourself and respond.

In your response to the discussion question, you should express your own ideas. When expressing your ideas, it is important that you integrate what you have learned into your thinking. Discussions should be at least *seventy words* because it is very difficult to express, thoughtfully, any idea or concept in fewer words.

REACTIONS: (Feelings)

DISCUSSION QUESTION:

DISCUSSION:
(At least seventy words) Your *IDEAS!* Don't just repeat facts! *RESPOND* to them!)

# LEARNING SUMMARY FORM

Name _____
Class Time _____
Number _____
Date _____

## TOPICS AND SUBTOPICS COVERED

1. _____      6. _____
2. _____      7. _____
3. _____      8. _____
4. _____      9. _____
5. _____     10. _____

## LEARNINGS: (Facts, Thoughts, Ideas, Concepts)

1. _____

   _____

2. _____

   _____

3. _____

   _____

4. _____

   _____

5. _____

   _____

6. _____

   _____

7. _____

   _____

8. _____

   _____

9. _____

**REACTIONS: (Feelings)**

**DISCUSSION QUESTION:**

DISCUSSION (At least seventy words) Your *IDEAS!* Don't just repeat facts! RESPOND to them!)

# LEARNING REVIEW

Name _____

Date _____

Class _____

List major topics studied in class and indicate the date on which they were discussed.

| **Major Topics Studied** | **Date Presented** |
|---|---|
| 1. _____ | _____ |
| 2. _____ | _____ |
| 3. _____ | _____ |
| 4. _____ | _____ |
| 5. _____ | _____ |
| 6. _____ | _____ |
| 7. _____ | _____ |
| 8. _____ | _____ |
| 9. _____ | _____ |
| 10. _____ | _____ |
| 11. _____ | _____ |
| 12. _____ | _____ |
| 13. _____ | _____ |
| 14. _____ | _____ |
| 15. _____ | _____ |
| 16. _____ | _____ |
| 17. _____ | _____ |
| 18. _____ | _____ |
| 19. _____ | _____ |
| 20. _____ | _____ |
| 21. _____ | _____ |
| 22. _____ | _____ |
| 23. _____ | _____ |
| 24. _____ | _____ |

When you consider the topics and activities that you feel you learned most from, you will be able to summarize your learnings and your reactions to them. The learnings may be related to your personal growth, rather than to the topics themselves.

Which topics were of most interest to you?

1. _____
2. _____
3. _____
4. _____
5. _____
Why? _____
_____
_____
_____
_____

Which topics were of least interest to you?

1. _____
2. _____
3. _____
4. _____
5. _____
Why? _____
_____
_____
_____
_____

From which class sessions did you learn the most?

1. _____
2. _____
3. _____
4. _____
5. _____

Why?

_____
_____
_____
_____
_____

What was the one most important learning you gained in this course?

## FINAL DISCUSSION QUESTIONS:

Teachers may identify two questions that will provide students an opportunity to explore, conceptualize and express their thinking about the major issues and concepts of the course. Teachers may wish to have students identify two questions and respond to them.

**Discussion Question I.**

**Response: (At least one hundred and forty words)**

**Discussion Question II.**

**Response: (At least one hundred and forty words)**

If a learning surprised you, explain why and in what way.

In rethinking your views on an issue, comment on the manner in which you changed your opinion.

If the learnings had meaning for you as a person, explore the possibility that you may have changed, appraise the change and tell how you feel about it.

List books and readings that have contributed to your learning. These include hand-outs and assigned materials.

Any other comments?
(Under comments, give suggestions that you feel would make using the Learning Review more helpful. Offer your ideas about the use of time in class, for instance, or any feelings, positive or negative, about the class. Feel free to evaluate the teacher.

# Browsing Bibliography

Crystal, John C. and Richard N. Bolles. *Where Do I Go from Here with My Life?* Berkeley: Ten Speed Press, 1974.
Life and career planning.

Ford, George A. and Gordon Lippitt. *Planning Your Future.* La Jolla: University Associates, 1972.

Gelatt, H. B., Barbara Varenhorst, Richard Carey, and Gordon P. Miller. *Decisions and Outcomes.* Princeton: College Entrance Examination Board, 1973.
Exercises in decision making.

Gordon, Thomas. *P. E. T.: Parent Effectiveness Training.* New York: New American Library, 1975.

Isgar, Tom and Susan. *Learning Games.* Washington, D.C.: United States National Student Association, no date.
Introduction to role playing and how to lead it.

Koch, Kenneth. *I Never Told Anybody. Teaching Poetry in a Nursing Home.* New York: Random House, 1977.
———. *Rose, Where Did You Get That Red? Teaching Great Poetry to Children.* New York: Random House, 1973.
———. *Wishes, Lies and Dreams: Teaching Children To Write Poetry.* New York: Vintage Books, 1970.

LeShan, Lawrence. *How To Meditate: A Guide to Self-Discovery.* New York: Bantam Books, 1975.

Lewis, Howard R. and Harold S. Streitfeld. *Growth Games: How To Tune In Yourself, Your Family, Your Friends.* New York: Bantam Books, 1972.

Lyons, Gracie. *Constructive Criticism.* Berkeley: Issues in Radical Therapy, 1976..

Miller, Sherod, Elam W. Nunnally, and Daniel B. Wackman. *Alive and Aware: How To Improve Your Relationships Through Better Communication.* Minneapolis: Interpersonal Communication Programs, Inc. 1975.

Panzarella, Andrew. *Microcosm, A Radical Experiment in Re-Education for Becoming a Person.* Winona, Minn.: St. Mary's College Press, 1972.

Parnes, Sidney J. *Creative Behavior Guidebook.* New York: Scribner's, 1967.
Exercises in imaginal skills.

Perls, Fritz S. *Gestalt Therapy Verbatim.* New York: Bantam Books, 1972.

Pfeiffer, J. William and John E. Jones. *A Handbook of Structured Experiences for Human Relations Training,* Vol. I. La Jolla: University Associates, 1969.
———. *The 1980 Annual Handbook for Group Facilitators.* San Diego: University Associates, 1980.
See also *Annuals* for 1972–1979; 1981.

Satir, Virginia. *Making Contact.* Millbrae, Cal.: Celestial Arts, 1976.
Interpersonal communication and self-esteem.
———. *Peoplemaking.* Palo Alto: Science and Behavior Books, 1972.

Sax, Seville and Sandra Hollander. *Reality Games: Games People Ought To Play.* New York: Popular Library, 1972.

Simon, Sidney B., Leland W. Howe and Howard Kirschenbaum. *Values Clarification: A Handbook of Practical Strategies for Teachers and Students.* New York: Hart Publishing Co., 1972.

Stevens, John O. *Awareness, Exploring, Experimenting, Experiencing.* Moab, Utah: Real People Press, 1971.

Torrance, E. Paul. *Torrance Tests of Creative Thinking.* Princeton: Personal Press, Inc., 1966.